(((((Gene ᴜ₁))))) Broadcast

The life and insight of the ambulance frontline

DARREN JENSEN

Dedicated to my Grandmother

First published in 2022 in the United Kingdom by
DARREN JENSEN
Southend-on-Sea, Essex, UK

Text & images © 2021 Darren Jensen

ISBN 978-1-3999-3382-7

ACKNOWLEDGEMENTS
The inspiration to write this book followed a long battle with poor mental health. The stories within it have provided me with a good understanding of events that have taken place and a therapy that has led to a road of recovery.
I would especially like to thanks my partner, as well as my family, friends and colleagues who gave me the support to write this book. It has been a real pleasure to write and reflect upon my journey and, in doing so, my colleagues have been incredible in helping me to do this.
A percentage of the proceeds from the sales of this book will be donated to The Ambulance Staff Charity (TASC). For more information go to: www.theasc.org.uk

***

'*General broadcast*' is a phrase used in a control room and is an 'open mic' call over a radio system for all emergency crews to hear. Usually, ambulance crews are contacted 'one-to-one' by the control room.

***

Book production by

GABRIEL BOOKS
www.gabrielbooks.co.uk
info@gabrielbooks.co.uk

Cover design by Nick Snode
Typeset in Cronos 12/14pt and DIN Condensed Bold 24pt
Printed and bound by 4 Edge Limited / www.4edge.co.uk

Contents

Foreword

I COME FROM A WORK background in security and property management and grew up in a household where I had an exposure to what it was like to live with the disabled. It was partly from this experience that inspired a dream and a calling to work in pre-hospital care and, after a great deal of thought and reflection, I finally took the plunge to reach my dream.

With many highs as well as lows, I will take you on a journey of some incredible stories, laughter, tears, along with some real shock factors.

I dedicate this book to my late grandmother and to all of my colleagues that have sadly lost their lives – welcome to General Broadcast.

When we change the way we look at things,
the things we look at change.

Dr Wayne Dyer

1 | The Calling

IT IS SOMETIMES DIFFICULT to comprehend the wailing of a siren out in the distance, the sound of a clock ticking whilst you see an ambulance speeding past. Yet, the thought of someone desperately in need of help with what can seem like a typical day, can change in the blink of an eye.

Do you remember when you were young, people would often say to you; what do you want to be when you grow up. Followed by the typical responses of "I want to be a doctor, I want to be a policeman", occasions like this clearly show the hopes and dreams of a child.

When I was young, I don't believe I ever really knew what I wanted to do, well, not until I was around eight or nine years old. I began to have a sense of direction to things that I had a keen interest in, giving me a broader outlook towards the future.

The town we grew up in put on an air show every year and at these events the emergency services would display their vehicles where children would be allowed to climb around inside them.

I used to get very excited and count down the months until we got closer to the event that happened each summer. Year by year the whole town, as well as people from far and wide, would attend.

Growing up was tough living in a low-income household. The normal things most children were able to do were not always the case for me. When I was around eleven my friend and I went out, one weekend, to look for a job. We eventually found ourselves down at the seafront. We made our way, one by one, to each seafood restaurant looking for whatever work we could get.

Sometime later we managed to get a job working in a kitchen. Simple work such as washing of plates and carrying boxes around to make money for what we wanted.

There was a massive fashion culture amongst children in the 1990s so now I could finally afford things such as trainers, a mountain bike, all the things that would make me fit in with my friends.

At this young age, I just knew that I had the ambition to be the best I could be with my positive outlook towards life.

My mum sent myself and my siblings to St John Ambulance to learn first aid as my sister had a serious epilepsy condition.

Most kids walk to school with their friends but I had to walk with my sister to make sure she got to school and help if she had a seizure. There was a hereditary disability within my family; the condition is known as HSP, 'Hereditary Spastic Paraplegia'. It presents itself in a similar way to MS but this condition only affects the legs. My mother would sometimes collect me from school and this could be difficult for me sometimes as kids of that age would love to bully. This bullying soon became the norm.

With considerable exposure at such a young age to medical conditions, I guess working in healthcare, in some shape or form in my life, was going to happen.

My first medical role was for a private ambulance company and the only role I could apply for was as an Ambulance Care Assistant. This was a good foundation as it entailed taking patients to and from their appointments. Within this role I began to hear lots of fantastic stories from patients of times gone by.

Typical stories would have been a time back in the war, where people would describe countries they had been to and how they served their country. Also stories of servicemen that had been invalided out of the forces such as Spitfire pilots, tank drivers, and even some recovering patients who assisted in making ammunition in the factories. You couldn't help but feel privileged to have these conversations with them, as you could see that they really enjoyed telling them.

A few years later I was approached to see if I was interested in attending a course to aid me in achieving the next level in medical care – an Emergency Care Assistant. This would enable me to work on a frontline ambulance alongside Emergency Medical Technicians (EMTs) and paramedics.

I was thrilled and gladly accepted; within a month or so, I carried out and completed the course and as scared as I was about the exams, I just knew it would be worth it.

To respond with an emergency ambulance, I needed to take a driving course that taught me how to do emergency driving. It was like taking my driving lessons all over again. You think that you know everything about how to drive when you pass your general driving test. Well, this advanced course really did open my eyes to the mistakes and complacency we can acquire over the years of driving on the roads.

This was later showed up quite clearly when I was able to work on frontline duties and respond to calls. The course taught me a safe way to drive including how to let other road users know that I needed to get past.

I really enjoyed working on the frontline but sometime later I knew that I wanted more. I wanted to not just be the driver and assistant but also be a medic that aids and treats the patient.

I needed a time of reflection to think about the direction I should take in my career. After some careful consideration, and with nerves at a high,

I signed up for a course to become an EMT (Emergency Medical Technician). The course was not easy but no matter how tough it got I just knew I needed to pass.

The course had a massive financial impact on our family. Without the support from my partner, whilst I studied, I doubt I could have ever have achieved what I did.

Revision and more revision... If I thought that the previous courses had been tough, this one proved to be a lot harder but I persevered. The wait, after the course, was tense but I could not have been happier when the results were in – "I passed". Finally the future of my career was starting to take shape.

My first day out I was a bag of nerves. It does not matter how many times you practice things in a classroom, when it comes down to treating a real patient you will never forget the anxiety and apprehension of taking part in a 'real life' medical emergency.

My Nan has always been an important part in my life and as time moved on I managed to visit her often as she lived just across the road from us. I always enjoyed spending half of the summer holidays at her home especially when she always cooked some lovely treats that we shared whilst watching a good movie.

She would often ask how I was getting on and it became clear that she had thought I had been working for the NHS all of these years and not the private industry that subcontracted for them.

There's always a sense of pride when wearing a uniform... the logo that's boldly displayed on your chest that highlights the work you do in the community but to have the letters of NHS on my uniform would of course be amazing. I remember my Nan telling me about how she remembered the NHS being formed, this was part of her time in history. Things were so different back then, people were not shy to work hard in difficult times and to support and encourage one another.

The more I thought about it, the more I knew I wanted to join the NHS. I searched around online, hunting for that one position that would get my foot in the door.

One day whilst sitting at the table with my laptop I saw a position for a qualified EMT, checking the rest of the advert I saw it was local and full time, so I applied.

Within a few days I got a reply, I was invited to an interview. To say how nervous I was, and that my hands shook, would be hard to put into words but it was now time for me to take the plunge.

I arrived at the ambulance station and was invited to sit a written paper, thirty questions all regarding my role. It didn't take long. I then realised that there would also be interview with a panel of three paramedics. Each member was lovely and put me at my ease. We concluded the interview with a shake of the hands – I remembered my grandfather always telling me that you can tell a lot from a man by the shake of his hand, firm grip, but not too tight – after shaking hands I was advised that they would be in touch.

It seemed like weeks that I had to wait... Every day the mailman arrived, I would be at the door like an expectant kid at Christmas waiting for his presents. Finally the letter came.

I remember the feeling of excitement as I opened the letter that told me I had been successful. A huge amount of emotion came over me, along with a heightened sense of excitement at the same time.

A few weeks passed, I had to go and be sized up for a uniform. I felt so excited to be able to move forward, and finally start the job that I had always dreamed of doing.

I still remember the feel of the box that was placed in my hands and the smell of the shining leather boots as I opened the packaging – this is it, I thought to myself, I really am going to become a paramedic. What was once, simply a childhood dream, was now in fact becoming a reality.

I tried on the uniform many times in front of the mirror and as I looked at myself childhood memories formulated in my mind.

I often talked to my Nan about my aspirations and she always told me that I can be whatever I wanted to be – I had just got to want it enough and believe in myself. I had been keeping my job application a secret as I had this awful fear of jinxing things. However, that the fear was now in the past, it had been replaced with a huge excitement as I knocked on her door and waited there in my new uniform.

As my nan was disabled, many paramedics used to attend and assist her from time to time but now she was taken aback and did what seemed like a triple take... After a few moments I could see the recollection on her face as she suddenly realised that this time it was me standing there in the uniform. A beaming smile spread across her face followed by a burst of excitement. She congratulated me and said, "See, I told you, anything is possible".

The job itself taught me, at a very early stage, that it is easy to take things for granted in life. What can seem like a normal day can quickly turn into your worst nightmare, changing not only your own day-day life but also that of those around you.

It seemed as though time went incredibly slowly the day before my first shift. I remember inspecting my uniform and checking several times all my equipment was ready. As the evening dragged on I sat there for several hours cleaning and shining my boots, being brand new they weren't even dirty but I was so keen to make a good impression on my first day.

My alarm was set followed up by a second alarm. My intention was to have an early night but it was difficult to get to sleep as I was apprehensive and many thoughts whizzed around in my head. I said to myself, "This is it, time to make a difference". Just as I was getting settled, I decided to ring my nan to tell her what was happening the next day, she told me that I would have the best day, as after all, they have her grandson to look after them. With those heartfelt words I drifted off to sleep.

Dawn broke, a new day... Beams of sunlight slowly illuminated the room as my eyes adjusted to the light. I was already awake before the alarm had a chance to kick in, what was meant to be a good quota of sleep definitely felt nowhere near the amount needed.

I slowly got dressed and checked everything over and over again. I looked back into the mirror and remember thinking to myself how smart I looked and how chuffed I was to wear the uniform.

It seemed as if there was no traffic at all on the road as I made my way to the station. Approaching the security barrier I attempted to make my way into the yard. It didn't work, trying again and again still no joy, I pressed the buzzer anxiously awaiting a response, this faint voice asked if they could help me. After gaining entry I searched for an available space to park the car, settling for the first available spot. I grabbed my kit and nervously made my way inside.

The first door I saw, as I entered, said 'Duty Manager'. I will never forget the feel and sound of my sweaty hands as my knuckles wrapped on the door. A voice responded "come in", I pushed the door open and was met with a happy welcoming smile as I introduced myself.

I had only been there a matter of a few hours when the training room door swung open and a manager bellowed, "Does anyone own a car with the following registration", it was me, I remember panicking as already something was going wrong.

It turned out that not only had I parked in the wrong space, I had also parked in the spot that was allocated for the duty manager's response car. I must have apologised at least six times but it was all met with a lot of banter which helped ease my nervousness for the rest of the day.

I had a few assessments to carry out but before I could start these I had to frequent the men's toilets many times! To the people around me it must have looked like I was a man with bladder problems. I couldn't slow down my nerves. I heard my name being called and slowly approached the assessment room.

I was given a straight forward scenario of a gentleman with chest pain. The assessment itself was going really well, right up until I was thrown a curve ball. The instructor told me that my patient has just gone into cardiac arrest.

My hands began to sweat badly and I could feel my breathing begin to rise. I kept saying to myself, "Think Darren think, get it together". I had been training for this for a long time, I reeled myself back in my mind. What was only a matter of seconds seemed like several minutes. I completed the scenario, the best I could, and anxiously awaited the results.

The day itself went so quickly. After a lunch break I returned to the classroom to find an envelope on my table. Expectant to know what was inside, I slowly peeled back the seal to reveal an A4 sheet of paper. As my eyes adjusted to the small text, I shouted with excitement – I had passed!

I thought to myself, well that's stage one out of the way, now for the big hurdle of a driving assessment this afternoon. It's strange to think about what can make one nervous, something as simple as driving which you do on a day-day basis can put the fear of God into you.

It was only a short drive to the assessment centre and when I arrived I made sure that I didn't make the same mistake with the parking spaces. With understandable apprehension and rising nervousness I wondered how many mistakes that I had already made.

I signed myself into the visitor's log and took my place in the waiting room. It didn't take long for my name to be called and as I walked outside I was first asked to read the number plate in front of me. As I did so, I could see a female member of staff walking back to her car in tears. She was on her phone and was talking loudly enough for me to hear her say that she had failed.

I carried out my safety checks and followed the instructions of the assessor who was really nice. He asked for me to drive through the town on busy urban roads as well as dual carriageways and motorways. The test itself took around thirty minutes, I returned to the assessment centre and parked the vehicle up. The next few minutes of silence seemed like forever but then a hand reached out to me from the passenger seat, followed by the assessor saying, "Congratulations", with a smile on his face.

The following days and months went quickly and it was not long before I was ready to go out and face the community and to do what I signed up for.

I had a few days off before I could start but as you can imagine I couldn't rest. I now had a new kind of excitement in view of actually going out on the road. The days past and it was important to make sure I had some good rest as other people I knew in the industry had always told me how rare it was to get some good down time.

With minutes turning into hours, and hours into days, the day finally approached – life began on the frontline.

Some wake up to an alarm,
others wake up to a calling.

(Unknown)

2 | Self-reflection

After being in the service for just a few of weeks, I took some time to look back at some of the jobs as well as stories I had encountered along the way...

My very first day out on the road was actually on Remembrance Day and being from a family that has a military background, I have always been keen to listen to war time stories from the old days. I am not sure if it was just because life was so different back then or the huge sacrifices of the older generation, either way it always gives me pleasure in taking the time to listen to their experiences.

The first few jobs were nice and straight forward, ongoing abdominal pain, urine infections, all the simple run-of-the-mill jobs that the service encounters. That said, what is in fact a simple straight forward job to us, can actually be the worst point in time for the patient.

We were on our way to another job when all of a sudden, the radio went off from control, this only happens one of two ways, (1) if we call and they answer, or (2) if they are in need of urgent assistance for a confirmed or suspected life and death call.

The radio bellowed, sending a cold shudder down my spine as the controller transmitted, "General broadcast, general broadcast". The call was for a 94-year-old man who was unconscious. As the lights were activated, I had all sorts of thoughts running through my head. This was my very first category one call, and my mind was running away with me thinking of what I could expect when we arrived at the scene.

We approached the house and were greeted by a carer, she explained that she was assisting the patient to get dressed when he fell back and smacked his head.

As I made my way to the bedroom, I was greeted by a pool of blood on the door frame, a shiver went through me as I pushed the door back and discovered our patient on the floor.

I called out immediately hoping to receive a response, "He's alive I thought to myself". He looked at me with a smile as I began to assess his injuries. After completing all the necessary checks and treating his wounds, my patient began to tell me that he was trying to get dressed in his suit. He wanted to sit in front of the TV and watch some of his comrades who were walking in the Remembrance Day parade.

As I looked around the room, I could see lots of memorabilia dating back to when he was in the war. I wasn't sure what to break to him first, the fact that his suit was ruined of the fact that he was going to require stitches at the hospital.

We managed to get a clean set of clothes on him, it was at this point he looked at me and said, "I'm not going to see the parade am I", my heart sunk, this man had given so much to society and that the one day that meant the world to him was not going to happen.

I told him that if we go now, we can quickly arrange for the hospital to return him home. Although upset, he agreed and we made our way to A&E. The journey didn't take that long but during this time he began to tell me where he had been stationed and spoke to me about his experiences in World War II. I remember thinking to myself, that in twenty years' time we are, unfortunately, going to lose all of this generation.

When we got to the hospital, I handed over my patient. He shook my hand and thanked us for our help and we returned to the vehicle and onto our next job. I'm not sure why but I couldn't seem to shift this job from my thoughts.

It was at around 10:30am when we returned to the hospital with another patient. As I was booking in, I looked across the 'major's' department and could see our previous patient sitting up in bed. He looked really upset sitting there, you could feel the weight of the world on his shoulders, I approached and said hello again, he looked up and smiled – it was then I suddenly had an idea.

I had a brass Remembrance Day pin badge on my uniform, I took it off and pinned it to his clothes, he said to me, "What's this?", I went on to explain that if he can't be at home and watch the parade, I am going to bring it to him.

The doctor came in to close up his wound. It was at this time I called my crewmate and explained what I was going to do. I used the opportunity, as I stood next to the old gentleman, to use my phone to play the live parade so he could watch a brief period of it whilst his head was being attended to.

I will never forget the tear that ran down his face, to this day I am unsure if it was from sadness of recollection of times gone by or because he was able to watch some of the broadcast. They always say that some jobs stay with you, for me this will be one that I would remember for a very long time.

I have learnt, as time moves on, that everyone has a story. We spend a fragment of time in someone's life but a few simple gestures of kindness can absolutely mean the world to them.

The rest of the day went well, back to straightforward jobs and other calls that you know did not require an ambulance. Some people call us as a last resort but we can tell that some patients should have received help sooner from GPs or community teams. It was calls for help like these that made it clear to me how stretched the service really is. We are often tied up with jobs at the end of our shift and do not finish on time due to making sure that patients have the right support after we leave.

After each shift you always take a little bit away from the day. It could be just thinking how thankful you are that you have your health or even just how much you went that extra mile. For me I know there will always be another job waiting, we just have to do our best for all the patients we encounter.

When you go home, tell them of us and say:
for your tomorrow we gave our today.

John Maxwell Edmonds

3 | Close to Home

YOU CAN WAKE UP SOME MORNINGS on a working day that seems like it's going to be a normal shift. It's easy to become complacent, to treat one day the same as the next.

Some time ago a paramedic, who had a long-distinguished service, told me that this is one of the most unpredictable jobs ever. I'm only now just remembering his words and that, in itself, shows how easy it is to forget.

It all seemed like a normal day, going to and from the hospital. Without a warning the radio blared, "General broadcast, general broadcast, C1 call". It is safe to say that the nature and description of these C1 category calls are not always as given. It can be frustrating at times the way the computer system, in the control room, triages the call.

The call was for a 17-year-old male with difficulty in breathing. We were only a few miles away so offered to go and assist. I had this overwhelming sense of uneasiness upon arriving at the scene. I wasn't sure why but nevertheless I had to get on with the job at hand.

My crewmate and I got all of the kit together and began to make our way to the house, we knocked but no answer. It is always worrying when this happens as you never know if the patient is alone or not. I knocked again and could hear footsteps running towards the door. We were greeted by what we later learnt was the patient's mother. She quickly led us to a downstairs bedroom where we found our patient who was seated on the end of the bed. His mother explained that he had developed a pain in his arm around six months before and, following some assessment, discovered that he unfortunately had cancer. This assessment was later followed up with surgery and later, thankfully, he got the all clear.

She went on to say, that after several months all seemed to be going well, then one day he began to have issues with his breathing, the cancer had returned, this time to both lungs.

Whilst the mother was relating this information, my crewmate had been assessing the patient. Just looking at him you could see he was struggling to breath properly. The vitals indicated that his oxygen levels were down, breathing rate was elevated, along with his heart rate slightly elevated too.

We discovered, that upon last discharge he had not received any follow up care, community care or even a referral. It was very evident that, since discharge, the family had been left in a kind of limbo, not knowing where to turn or even who to talk to.

Our priority was to stabilise our patient as much as possible, however, he made it very clear that he was not attending A&E. I advised him that he needed immediate treatment and, should he remain at home, he is likely to die. It's never a good feeling having to be brutally honest with a patient in that you have to tell them that they might die, but this job is all about being transparent in the way you deal with people as well as honest.

I was intrigued to know why he did not wish to attend. He told me that he had spent so much time in hospital that he could not face any more time there but it was clear to me what would happen should he remain at home.

The mother had distress written all over her face and it was obvious what the family had been going through – they clearly could not take any more.

We began giving nebulisers to ease his breathing. After his initial assessment it was imperative that he got to a place of definitive care, namely hospital. All the while this was going on, I could not help but think about just how young the patient was – he was a year older that my daughter. The thought of my own child being in the same or similar position was just unthinkable. It was at this point I could feel increasing waves of emotions come over me. I needed to distract myself and the only thing I could think of was to take the mother to one side and explore all options that we had available.

It became apparent that the last ward the patient was on was in fact a paediatric ward. I began to source the number and then gave them a call, this was with the view to bypassing A&E altogether.

I spoke to the nurse in charge, she said that due to the fact our patient had passed the threshold of his seventeenth birthday and that he now no longer fell under the responsibility of the paediatric team. However, she went on to give me the details of an adult ward that may be able to help.

I could feel myself becoming more and more frustrated, not only because I felt that I was becoming emotionally attached to the job, but more so for the family as they had been so badly failed and overlooked by the system.

I called the ward with the details that I had been given. Well, this turned out to be worse than the previous call, they contradicted all the prior information stating he should still be under paediatrics. I was dreading having to relay all this information, I knew that my mental bandwidth was becoming more and more narrow, along with knowing that we only had a limited amount of oxygen on the vehicle.

With nobody willing to accept our patient, as well as being told by the patient that A&E was off the table, all I could think of to do was pre-alert straight to the resus department. The resuscitation suite is where patients go that are in a life and death situation or in a rapidly unstable condition.

Knowing that his breathing was becoming more and more difficult, I had to propose the only option left available. He seemed to accept just how bad he had become and almost to the point where he knew that he would die within a short space of time.

I discussed our only option. What was said next will stay with me for a very long time, if not forever. I told him what had to be done and he looked at me and said, "I don't want to go to hospital but don't want to die either, promise me if I do go to hospital that I won't die there, I want to die at home".

I asked his mother if he had a DNAR (Do Not Attempt Resuscitation) form. These are normally put in place when a patient is terminally ill or will eventually require palliative care.

I discovered that a DNAR had been put in place, however since diagnosis, and even since last discharge, there had been no GP referrals or even any community action of any kind. It was if the patient and his family had been left out in the cold and in a kind of limbo. I couldn't help but sense the frustration. Along with the emotion that was building in the room, it was very clear that the mother had been doing all she can to support her son – she was doing all the natural things that a mother would do.
As she ran through a few things with me, surrounding his diagnosis, I could sense, in a weird kind of way, that it was as if she had been picturing this day for some time to come but also, understandably, trying to distract herself from the harsh reality that faced her each day.

It must have been so difficult for her, as when I asked her about prior support from her GP, she said that it had been impossible to get through to the surgery, let alone getting an appointment. As I started to understand how difficult this time had been for them, I still could not help but picture my daughters face, fearing that in a blink of an eye, it could have been her. One-minute things are fine, we go about our daily lives, making plans with hopes and dreams for the future and then next minute your world can come crashing down.

When you realise how much a family can be let down by the system, this can often highlight the importance of the uniform you wear and the obligation you have to ensure that your patient receives the best possible level of care.

We had given back-to-back nebulisers the whole time on scene and were mindful as to how much oxygen we had remaining. The journey to the hospital would only take around ten minutes, and as we began to get ourselves ready, the patient completely broke down. The fear of what could happen to him had come close to the forefront of his mind.

It only took a few minutes to get to the ambulance but it seemed to take ages. We were glad to finally be on our way. I had called ahead to the hospital about our concerns – this in the service is known as a pre-alert, we call and advice as to the nature of the patient's condition along with all relevant vital information.

Whilst keeping our patient as stable as we could, his observations began to deteriorate. I looked out of the window to give myself an idea of how far away we were. I estimated we were just over a minute away. I looked at my patient to try and give some level of assurance that we were nearly there. As we arrived, I could feel the pit of my stomach begin to churn, I believe this was more for the reason of knowing that the outcome was not looking positive at all.

We entered the resus department where a full handover to the consultant was made. As I held the young lad's hand and began to say goodbye, he thanked us for our help but I could see the fear in his face that looked back at me. That face would stay with me forever.

I was due some rest for the next three days. Despite having time off I couldn't help but dwell on what the possible outcome might be for the young guy. The days past and morning broke on my next scheduled shift. As I drove to work I contemplated on when I would be able to get an update surrounding my last job.

As we entered the hospital the next day I spotted a member of staff from the previous night and asked if there was any update regarding our patient. They didn't have to say anything as the look they gave us answered our question. They told us that at around 3:30am he had sadly passed away. At that moment a world of emotions came over me along with so many questions about my clinical practice.

Had I done enough? Could I have convinced him to go to hospital sooner? I knew that all of the questions I began to ask myself would not bring him back. We may only be ambulance staff, but we are humans as well and it became evident that something needed to be done to help others in a similar situation.

The management team had been informed about the young guy passing away, and when we returned to the station, later that day, we were told that a manager wanted to speak to us. As we spoke to him we could see that he was a very experienced member of staff and listened carefully to what we said. We mentioned that it would have been helpful if there had been a separate alert line to assist crews who are dealing with paediatrics, or even those who have a complex transition from paediatric to adult care medical history.

A few days later I arrived at the station to start my shift, and as I was walking out to collect my vehicle, a manager tapped me on the shoulder. I looked around to be handed a piece of paper. He said to me, "You may need this", "and you may be interested to know this is off the back of a job you did and a few other crews".

I looked down at the piece of paper to see a phone number with the words 'Paediatric Alert Line' next to it. I was instantly taken aback, and said, "What's all this about?"

He explained that following the very difficult nature of the job I had been involved with, that hospital management had called a meeting to discuss trying to improve patient care. The conclusion of the meeting was that the frontline crews need better access to hospital rapid intervention and to be better prepared to assist with such difficult jobs that we had been involved with.

That early call will enable a team of appropriate doctors and nurses to be ready on standby, to assist patients in such a predicament moving forward.

For me, I know it doesn't bring my patient back, but I have now been able to get some closure, knowing that other patient's as well as crews can be better prepared and treated in the future.

Not everything that is faced can be changed,
but nothing can be changed until it is faced.

James Baldwin

4 | Uniforms and Rainbows

MOST OF US CAN REMEMBER stories that our elders used to tell us as we were growing up, the war, the recession as well as many others. None of us would have ever of thought that in our lifetime we would be living through a pandemic – a story that in years to come we would speak about with our own children and grandchildren.

My shifts were passing by week-by-week and all seemed to carry on the same as it did every other day. That was until, whilst on station having a break, we all began to talk about the fact that many of us had been coming across patients whose oxygen saturations were in the 70's although still managing to speak without difficulty. In the medical field a person's oxygen levels are measured out of 100%, any patient with oxygen levels of around 94%, with no respiratory history, would normally feel short of breath. Anything lower and you know that they would find it hard to speak a sentence without distress.

Patients with these symptoms were presenting more and more often but it didn't make any sense to us. Something was not right. It was around November in 2019 that many people with breathing difficulties were being sent an ambulance, along with some who had conditions such as COPD. We began to see symptoms which all looked like chest infections, however, these cases were worse than any of us had seen before.

Persistent cough, raging temperature, low oxygen levels, all of this with flu-like symptoms on top. Within a week the news was on the TV about a virus that had escaped from a lab in China.

As an ambulance service we were not prepared for anything like this. Originally, we were just given surgical masks but there were not enough to go around. It was not uncommon, on a normal day, that we would attend five to six patients with breathing problems but then the numbers started going through the roof.

The thought of going to work, and that this virus was so infectious, was worrying and apprehension began to rise within the staff. I was dreading catching it, let alone passing it on. Aprons were beginning to be supplied to staff but these were so thin that even the smallest amount of wind blew them up in the air hitting us in the face.

My first thoughts were, is the apron contaminated and have I just potentially infected myself? I knew that any protection was better than none, but the potential daily risks to us began to mount along with the understandable anxiety that came with it.

Within a month I began to feel unwell. I had a headache and no matter what I did or took for it, I was just unable to get rid of it. I also had a sore throat that was worse than any I have had in my life. Family, friends, as well as several members of staff all started to fall ill.

My household seemed to get wiped out in just one day. Was it me? Did I just infect the whole house from the work I did in treating my patients? I had been so careful, showering at work, cleaning everything that I could possibly think of.

I had to self-isolate and, the time I spent doing this, seemed like an eternity which just made me overthink everything. Finances began to get difficult and bills slowly started to mount up. It came to the point where I had to make calls to utility providers to help me with sorting out my payments. This was the last thing I had expected to do but everyone I spoke to were very understanding and it was nice to feel supported.

They had obviously had a considerable amount of similar calls as mine as the Covid virus had contributed to many people's money problems.

Within about five days my symptoms just vanished overnight. Everything had completely gone. It was good to feel better although all the rest of my household were still really ill.

Fortunately after ten days, or so, we were all starting to feel better and closer to normality – still not perfect but a world apart from where we were a short time before. Some of the symptoms still remained but this seemed to be a normal factor with the virus.

I had to remain at home and keep the family safe but the more I watched the news the more I could see the world falling apart and the hospitals at breaking point.

On my first day back I discovered that around thirty percent of the frontline workforce were off sick. Precautions were also at an all-time high for everyone. Instructions were being given about new signs and symptoms of the virus, pretty much all who had the symptoms had to go to hospital.

We began to take many patients, who had contracted the virus, to hospital. The view as we entered the grounds stood out like a landmark that clearly reflected the state of the country as well as the NHS. From the entrance ramp, right up to the hospital doors, there was row after row of ambulances waiting to offload patients. We were told that if there was no space in the A&E department we had to remain on the ambulance with our patient. All the ambulances were illuminated with their hazard lights flashing which is an indicator that the patient was waiting to go inside, but due to no space they had to remain on the ambulance. We have never been shy of finishing late, but with the longest wait being over four hours, this just struck you with the sudden realisation how 'on its knees' the hospital was.

They still had the everyday patient's walking in to A&E – patient's that had the ability to seek help and support from their GP or even a pharmacy. I completely understand that when a patient needs help, it is 'their emergency', but we would often get less important call outs such as someone who had been experiencing back pain for six months and then at 2.00am calls for an ambulance to say they were still in pain.

Calls such as that really do put things into perspective, but you still have to remember where you are and treat the patient with the upmost professionalism.

As much as we wanted to attend and help the sickest of patients, the hospitals were beginning to run low on oxygen. It came to a point where we could not give oxygen to patients with levels that remained at 94%, and supplies were starting to be withdrawn. This hit us all like a brick, the country, as well as the world, was on its knees. The media didn't help; there were so many mixed messages out there and wrong information being given out. The government were telling the public that it was not as bad as people were being told but all the while, the key workers, knew a different story.

The public would see us arrive at an incident in our white protective body suits, whilst they stood at their doors, looking at us, to get a glimpse of someone else's misfortune. Photos and videos were being posted on social media, that started to raise awareness of the true situation and re-enforced everyone's opinion of what really was going on in the world.

Attending a cardiac arrest would be the worst – hot weather, thick uniform, respirator, goggles and panicking that the patient was infected with Covid whilst you did compressions on their chest.

Some days you would drive home from work and see people out in groups, such as bank holiday street parties. All of these things we observed and compared it to the day we had just endured.

The fear of taking back a virus to your home was a really scary thought. Doing your bit for your country, whilst still trying to keep your family safe, is no easy task. When you get into this job, you know there is a risk to your own safety, but nothing humanly possible could prepare anyone for a pandemic.

With staff falling sick, you can't help but worry and think: 'Is it me next?' 'Am I going to catch it?' and then, as well all of these fears, you get thrown another curve ball, one that strikes so hard that it shakes the whole workforce.

All of us went about our day with the same jobs coming in and after a few months it seemed to be the new normal. I don't like that term but it is the easiest way to explain what it was like.

* * *

It was on one of those 'normal' days, and just after we had handed a patient over to A&E, that we were told that a colleague of ours had been hospitalised with Covid-19. It brought it home to us just how unwell they must have been to have to be hospitalised. As the day went on we learnt that they were not showing any signs of improvement. The situation was beginning to get serious. We had a message relayed to us, through another member of staff, that our colleague was going to be intubated but that they wanted to tell us, that we should all look after each other and they hope to see us all soon.

We were all shocked, this was the first time someone I knew was so unwell as a result of contracting the virus. As the days went on we received various messages that there was no improvement in his condition. The medical staff tried different methods of treatment but eventually a message was relayed from management that our colleague had passed away.

I couldn't comprehend the news, none of us could, our colleague was not only one of the nicest people you could wish to meet, they were also an outstanding paramedic too.

This was the first paramedic I knew, to unfortunately pass away, due to the virus. We already knew we had been coping with a tremendous amount of fear on a daily basis – this just upped it even further.

We would often take elderly patients to hospital that we could clearly see showed signs of the virus and we knew that, as they said goodbye to their husband or wife, there was a high probability that they would never see them again.
It is things like this that would also get to you emotionally, especially when you learnt that they had been married for fifty or sixty years and for most of that time had not spent a day apart.

As the virus spread and new restrictions were introduced, friends and relatives of patients were not allowed to travel with them in the ambulance. Although the hospitals were doing their best to minimise the spread of the virus, it didn't help us with the already heightened anxiety that some patients had. Many patients refused to go unless their husband, wife or child could travel with them.

It's a difficult message to deliver when you know that a patient with Covid is likely to die if they do not get hospital attention. It doesn't sit well on your conscience when they still refuse to go and choose to remain at home.

The pandemic has taught me a lot about myself. All we can hope is that it has also taught the public a lot about themselves.

After a while the spirits of the NHS staff and other key care workers were very much lifted by a public vote of appreciation by clapping on a Thursday evening at 6pm. Pictures of rainbows started to appear on people's windows and doors. This often gave us a sense of hope in the knowledge that the public knew just how difficult our job was, as well as a sensible attitude when deciding whether to ring 999 or not.

There is a fine balance when it comes to a medical emergency. On one side there are patients that are very poorly and need your immediate attention and on the other side patients with a long-term illness that choose a completely random time in the early hours of the morning to seek medical help. Sometimes you'd notice a car in the driveway so a relative could have easily driven them if required!

We try not to be cynical but it often raises the question, when we attend these patients, when they say, "It has been going on for six months".

I suppose the thing that changed our outlook was when the number of calls we received changed from four to six calls, to eight and sometimes ten per shift. Many people had to wait a long time for an answer or were put on hold when they dialled 999. The control room began to break the news to callers that it would be at least forty to forty-five minutes until they received an ambulance and some even had to wait a lot longer.

We discovered that some of the patients we attended had tested positive for Covid and had already been seen at the hospital but later sent home. Then there was a frequency of calls from patients with breathing difficulties that phoned 999 because they or their relative just wanted to be checked over.

We completely understand that patients can feel really unwell one minute, but be in a reasonably stable condition, then suddenly go downhill. However, for some of these calls there was nothing different in the way the patients presented. Some would categorically make it quite clear to us that they had to have a check over if we were not going to take them to hospital.

It became quite deflating attending these types of call outs, especially if it made you work several hours after your shift, then of course you had the long drive back to station before you drove home. What would be a typical twelve-hour shift was now, a not uncommon, fourteen to fifteen-hour day.

We often try to understand just why some people felt that their calls warranted a 999 response. For some time now it has been promoted in the media, as well as on the radio, about inappropriate use of the service. If we managed to see a reduction in calls, we would have greater resources to accommodate the people in greater need.

My colleagues and I have attended, on many occasions, patients that have dialled 999 up to twenty times per shift. Fortunately we now have a department in the control room that is designated to handle these types of call but, as you can imagine, this in itself highlights the problems we encounter on a day-to-day basis.

It is surprising to see some of the lengths people will go to call us out. I attended a patient some time ago who was known as a frequent caller. They would say that they did not want to go to hospital and every time we attended there was never anything wrong with them.
This patient knew just how much strain they were adding to the local resources and would walk to the local phone box or use a passer-by's

mobile phone to call us. We would try and get to the root cause of why they wanted us so much but this proved an impossible task. In their case it seemed to be a fascination, that if they called, we would come.

In the service we are very conscious of the 'boy who cried wolf' scenario but we dread that day, should something be seriously wrong, we didn't attend.

We always support each other on our shifts and after a time you can feel the build-up of tension for yourself and your crewmate. Sometimes the emotional breaking point can feel very close by.

Unfortunately we will have to learn to live with Covid-19, as the virus will probably be here to stay for a long time, but we can change our outlook on life and learn to live a different way. As my nan always said, "We got through two wars, all as a result of pulling together".

She unfortunately passed away a few months before the outbreak but in some ways I am glad she is no longer here. I would hate to see her go through what society has experienced in the last few years.

Some things are best kept as a memory.

Only from the heart can you touch the sky.

Rumi

5 | Docks and Disaster

NO MATTER how many years you have been in the job, you will, at some point, attend such an unusual job that it catches you completely off guard or even so obscure that it can leave you scratching your head.

From time to time, you might ask yourself where would be a really strange place for a medical emergency to happen? You might think of places such as, on a hillside, in a tree or stuck in a bathroom...

It was a bright summers day; the shift was going well, with my crew mate and I taking in the sun for brief periods between jobs. We were just finishing our lunch when the radio went off. Control called to see if we could assist in a category 1 emergency about three miles away.

We quickly made our way to the vehicle. As we approached the ambulance we heard the onboard screen activate with the key job details and where we had to go. The call was for a lady with breathing difficulties. We heard that the she was on a barge boat within a marina. Neither of us had ever attended a call in such a location, however, we quickly made our way there.

As we arrived, we were greeted by a man frantically waving his arms at the side of the road. We parked up close to the water's edge. As I collected our equipment from the rear of the ambulance, I turned around to see the man running off down the marina. The equipment we carry can be really heavy such as a defibrillator, oxygen tanks, as well as a lot of kit in a large grab bag. The sun was beating down on me as I ran as fast as I could to where the barge boat was and it seemed to take us a long time to get there.

As I approached I could see that there was a gap between the pontoon and the boat which was slowly rising and falling with the current and tide of the water. Gaining entry to the boat took quite a few minutes and we were concerned not to lose our balance as we reached out to climb aboard and get to the patient.

I could hear frantic screams from inside the boat, and as we entered what seemed to be a lounge area, I noticed our patient leaning forward struggling to breath. She was trying to explain that she could not get her breath and that she had a bad chest pain that was making her unable to sit still.

Anyone who has been unfortunate to experience serious breathing problems, and unable to get their breath, know it can be very scary. I was carrying out the usual vital checks when, all of a sudden, she held her chest, went rigid and started agonal breathing.

I could hear a faint siren in the distance. Within moments of moving her to the floor she went into cardiac arrest. So many things began to go through my mind as the shock pads were placed on the patient's chest.

As we started CPR I heard an almighty scream from the patient's family. This brought whole situation into a sharp reality as to what was actually taking place. We were on a narrow barge boat, in the water with a patient in cardiac arrest. When you say that out loud it is hard to get your head around.

As the minutes began to pass, more and more colleagues began to arrive to assist us. We relayed the information as to what had happened on our arrival, along with what had taken place while we had been there. The space in which we were carrying out the CPR was so small and tight, only three people could be in there at any one time which made management of the situation very difficult.

We were a joined by a HART team (Hazardous Area Response Team). They are designed to provide additional support for situations like this, as well as other major incidents like terror attacks.

It was my turn to carry out CPR. As I was doing this, in the cramped conditions, I started to have a strange feeling of looking at the situation from a different angle – like time had stood still for a brief moment. I snapped myself back into reality as we checked the patient's rhythm on the defibrillator.

The screen of the defibrillator indicated a pulse so I quickly checked to see if I could feel one. I felt a heartbeat against my fingers and gave a sigh of relief. This is a very critical stage in a cardiac arrest, the patient is very weak, and any sudden movement can completely change all of the hard work that had been carried out.

We have a term we use when we manage to get a patient's heart restarted known as a ROSC, 'Return Of Spontaneous Circulation' and you could sense the relief in the team in the room, as well as from the family who were waiting out on the deck of the boat.

The HART team now stepped in. I had no clue how they were intending on getting the patient out of the boat, all I knew was that she needed to be in hospital. They wrapped the patient in a type of a carrying device that scooped her off the floor but also enabled up to six people to be around it at any one time. Suddenly I heard the sound of a drill and could see one of the relatives taking out one of the windows of the boat. The plan was to pass her through the window and once out try to keep her as flat as possible while using ropes to assist in pulling her from the boat pontoon. Around five minutes later we finally had the patient on the stretcher and began to slowly make our way to the ambulance.

At this stage we reassessed the patient; this was to ensure if we need to do anything further before making our way to the hospital. Although we had managed to get the patient back to life, there is always that fear that something could go wrong and cause the patient to go back into cardiac arrest.

The journey to the hospital was a tense drive. We were cautious of every bump as we tried to make progress through the heavy traffic. It still amazes me today the way some people can react when they see an emergency vehicle heading towards them.

It seemed like it took an hour to get to the hospital but was in fact it was only fifteen minutes when we finally arrived and made our way inside to hand over our patient.

In coming days you couldn't help but talk about the job – it had been such a team effort that had managed to save that lady's life. I just hoped that she remained well and able to return back to her normal life.

Statistically the percentage of patients that survive hospital to discharge, following a cardiac arrest, is only 5 per cent so I really hoped that she was going to make it. A month or so had past and I bumped into the crewmate that I was working with that day and he told me that our patient had survived and was later sent home a week or so later. I could not have been happier. The cardiac arrest had taken place under such difficult circumstances, so it was amazing for it to have such a great outcome.

I was at home some days later when my phone rang, it was the ambulance station, this is strange I thought why are they calling on my day off?

It was my manager who told me that they had received a call from the lady that had survived and that she wanted to come and see us and say thank you. A whole world of emotion began to run through me, happiness, relief, as well as the feeling of a job well done.

A date for a meeting was arranged and it didn't take long to come around. I was drinking my tea as we sat on the ambulance station waiting when the door opened and in walked the lady. She sat down and said hello to everyone. She asked us if we could talk her through the job and it seemed to us as if this, in itself, was helping her to achieve closure of the reality that her heart had stopped for some time. It was an amazing feeling to be reunited with that lady that had been very ill and at her worst but was able to benefit from a team that worked at their best to save her life – a great effort all round.

If you create your life with love,
your dream becomes a masterpiece of art.

Miguel Angel Ruiz

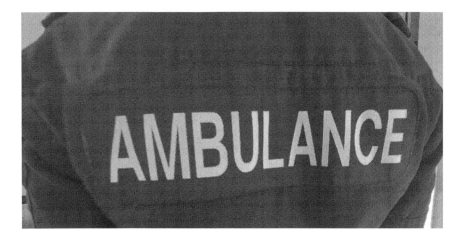

6 | Dead in the Water

HAVE YOU EVER BEEN in a situation where you think to yourself, 'what on earth was that person thinking?' The thing with this job is that you can guarantee, that when some people say you have seen everything, you can bet your bottom dollar, you really haven't.

My crewmate and I were roughly a quarter of the way through our shift when a call came over the radio for immediate assistance. A community nurse was on scene with a patient with a rare condition that meant that their oxygen saturations always sat lower than normal.

The patient had recently developed a chest infection and had begun to deteriorate quickly over the last forty-eight hours. This meant that, with already low oxygen levels, the patient could become a time critical emergency.

The patient's street was like most of the roads in the area with staggered cars parked on either side and some that were double parked. It was a long road and we started to look out for the door numbers. There was a vehicle approaching us from the other direction but when he saw our blue lights slowed down and flashed his lights for us to pass. As we set off to move through, another car overtook the vehicle that had slowed down in front of us and began to push through between us and the other vehicle.

With our vehicle being so large, and the parked cars blocking other parts of the road, there was no way that this car could get through.

We lowered the window and began to speak to the driver who looked to be in his early twenties. He instantly responded with verbal abuse telling us to move our bloody ambulance out of his way. We started to plead with him explaining that we were on our way to a really sick child but this had absolutely no effect on the driver at all. Our words were lost on him and he just shouted more verbal abuse back at us – this time of a racist nature.

The minutes began to pass and we were at a standoff. He was still refusing to budge. We could not move backwards as the traffic behind us had begun to build up and even if we could have done so the tight manoeuvring of the ambulance would have made it impossible.

I looked up the road ahead and there were no other vehicles behind him except the car he had overtaken. The driver of that car now got out of his vehicle and began to shout at the driver telling him to move out of the way.

With further insults, the driver put his car in reverse and screeched backwards allowing us to pass. It didn't end there, as we started to pass his car, he then decided to spit at us which came through the window hitting my crewmate.

By now we had lost so much time. I had already made a note his registration number and we intended to report his disgraceful behaviour to the police after we had helped the child we were trying to attend.

We finally pulled up at the address, grabbed our kit and ran to the door. The child looked really poorly and there was no time to waste.

We waited a short while as the nurse relayed the information on the condition of the child along with her vital observations.

My crewmate went back to the ambulance to get it ready for the patient and mother. As we left the house to join him, he said to me, "Mate, we're going nowhere". Puzzled by this comment, I asked what he meant, he pointed to the rear nearside tyre, it had a huge slash in it.

A neighbour, who had been looking on, told us that a car had pulled up as we entered the address. A man had got out, slashed one of the ambulance tyres then got back in his car and sped off. I couldn't believe it, why would anyone do that?

My heart sank, along with an overwhelming sense of concern for the time critical patient. We could only give limited help to the child who needed urgent hospital care. We were completely 'dead in the water' with no way of leaving.

I called the control room and told them we needed another crew, and fast, as well as the police and the recovery service. Fortunately it was not long before we heard a siren in the distance and when they arrived we did a handover and off they went.

I gave a partial sigh of relief. The time critical factor of this job had turned into a nightmare but now was finally over – or at least that's what we thought.

The police arrived about ten minutes later and parked behind the ambulance. The longer we were there, the more that people began to come out of their homes to see what was going on. Two ambulances as well as a police car – they must have been really curious.

We stood by the ambulance and discussed the damage. A neighbour confirmed our worst fears that the ambulance had been specifically targeted.

As my crewmate called control to request recovery I saw, out the corner of my eye, someone pointing at us from a car. I turned to look and it was the idiot who had blocked the ambulance in, only this time the car had more occupants.

It was if he had gone off to get friends and then come back to confront us at the patient's home. I was only glad that the patient and the mother were no longer with us. I couldn't forgive myself if they got harmed as a result of this man's stupidity.

He sat in his car and began shouting all sorts of horrible things from the junction across the street. As he got out of his car the police officer stepped out from behind the ambulance. It was if everything slowed down, the reality of what had taken place, as well as the events that were unfolding, all merged into one. This guy clearly had a grudge.

He charged towards us while his friends got out of the car who also started to run quickly in our direction. One by one they suddenly noticed the police officer who appeared from behind the ambulance and slowed down.

I had a horrible feeling in the pit of my stomach that seemed to get worse second by second. It was the realisation that here were four men wanting to do us harm but just one police officer that was clearly outnumbered. He must have come to the same conclusion we did because he reached for his radio to call for back up. Within only a few minutes several police vehicles entered the street. Finally this horrible man and his friends were going to be dealt with.

Two police officers grabbed him and pushed him against a fence. It was only after we heard the sound of the cuffs fastening around his wrists that we felt we could relax. His friends were ordered to disburse or risk being arrested.

Everything had happened so fast but then it suddenly dawned on me that this man had a knife or some other kind of sharp instrument.

I looked back at the damage that had been caused and realised just how lucky we had been. A dangerous man had been taken off of the streets – well at least for a short while.

The police put the guy in the rear of their car. One of the other police officers approached us and asked the strangest question. He asked if our vehicle was still driveable. With everything that had just taken place, I couldn't help but wonder why this was so relevant. He went on to say that it was a rough neighbourhood and that they couldn't guarantee our safety if we waited there too long on our own. The vehicle we were driving was a Mercedes ambulance, these have a twin-rear axle making it very stable and assists when reversing. With our safety still in jeopardy we agreed to limp the ambulance up the road to a safe spot to await recovery.

We waited for around an hour to be rescued. This for me had to be the longest hour ever as we continued to be vigilant, constantly looking around to see if anyone else was looking for us as a result of the man being arrested. A recovery vehicle finally arrived. They managed to change the tyre in the end rather than recover the vehicle. The police officer wanted a statement and requested that we attend the police station as soon as possible. When we got there we gave our statements then the officer explained the next steps of the procedure.

Around a week or so later my phone rang – a call from a withheld number. It was the police who wanted to advise us that the man was going to plead 'Not Guilty'. I could not speak for a moment and the brief silence was clearly picked up by the officer who went on to say that, despite his plea, the case will still go to court. I hung up the phone and instantly thought back to the events that had happened that day. I was kind of retracing my steps to see if at any point I had done anything wrong. I knew I hadn't, but still, you could not help but ask yourself the question anyway.

Some months passed when I received another call, this time from the Courts Service. They advised that the case was still going ahead and that they wanted to ask if I had any questions or concerns.

I told them that my crewmate and I were apprehensive of being in the same room as the man, as well as the possibility of him having his friends there on the day. The lady said that she will note down all our concerns and also inform the magistrate.

The day finally came to find out what would happen to the man that had caused so much trouble. We arrived at the court and went through security then on to book ourselves in as being present for the case.

As we made our way up the stairs, we looked across to the waiting room, it was then that we locked eyes with the man from that day. As we were in uniform we stood out from the rest of the crowd and it didn't take long for him to spot us. Within seconds we heard a wave of verbal abuse that was shouted back in our direction. He clearly was not happy, he must have been hoping that we wouldn't turn up to the case.

His friends also began to join in the shouting. There were six of them and two of us and the tension began to mount. Unbeknown to us the police officer, from that day, had also been seated in the room waiting to be called if required. He stood up and got between the man and us, along with a couple of other officers that were also present.

My crewmate and I got ushered in to a side room, which we later found out was especially reserved for witnesses who are waiting to be called to give evidence. As we sat and drank coffee, we could still hear the commotion out of the window below the room we were sitting in. The police had removed the man's friends and then we were advised that the guy had been called into court to have the case read out before the judge.

Some twenty minutes later the police officer, in the case, came to see us. He explained that, no sooner had we arrived, the defendant decided to change his plea to guilty. He was finally admitting to what he had done, a massive turn of events, finally justice was going to be served.

Some months beforehand the law had been changed by the government who had reviewed the law on obstructing and/or assaulting an emergency service worker. We were certain that, because of this change in the law, this man would now have this new-found justice imposed upon him.

Waiting for the case to finish seemed to take forever but finally the prosecutor came to tell us the outcome of the case. The judge had heard all of the evidence and after deliberating had decided that a suspended sentence would best suit the charge.

We could not believe it. This man had caused so much trouble, as well as potentially endangering the life of a child.

We were absolutely gutted with the outcome. Was this justice? Is this what our justice system has really come to?

We often hear about police officers involved in much less severe offences being given custodial sentences and yet this man was treated so lightly by the court system. For days I tried to get my head around the outcome, but no matter how often I tried, it would not change the outcome.

The only comfort I could get from all of this was to know, that after following up with the hospital about the patient, they went back home and made a full recovery.

I still find it hard to understand some people's violent and irrational behaviour. All I can hope is that at some time they might see what damage they are causing and hopefully change their ways.

It always seems impossible until it is done.

Nelson Mandela

My Nan and myself.

With my son.

Presenting the cheque for the Community Impact Scheme.

47

Sleeping out and raising money for the homeless shelter.

Chatting with John about his love of football.

Unexpected change of duties as a dog rescue team.

Graduation.

7 | Frozen Feet

IF YOU WERE TO ASK ANYONE in the emergency services, 'What would be one of the scariest situations you could be in?' I am sure that you would get back a stack of scenarios with a wide range of situations.

We all dread that day you have to hit the emergency button on the top of your radio. No matter whether you've pressed it, or hear the distress beacon activate on your radio, either way it sends a chill right through you. It is the one situation none of us want to be in.
I have been in the service for some time but not once have I had to press that button. From time to time I have heard the distress beacon go off, but with the number of people in the service, you would expect to hear it here and there.

When it does go off, everyone's radio hears the same transmission in real time and it is difficult to sit on your hands and not be able to do anything to help.

I have heard many accounts from colleagues, over the years, as they explained various difficult jobs they have had to attend to. You can see the fear and distress in their faces as they relive an incident in front of you in very graphic detail. Some members of staff have had the misfortune of going to several jobs like this in a short space of time. Call it bad luck, or even just an indicator as to how bad our society has become, either way we're only human and some jobs play on your mind and really do not sit well with you.

The amount of poor mental health has increased substantially over the last few decades and it is scary to see a large percentage of it is from workers in the emergency service who are diagnosed with PTSD from the exposure to the difficult and sometimes harrowing type of work they can encounter on a regular basis.

* * *

This particular day appeared to start off as normal as any other. We had been on duty for a few hours when we got called out to an incident that was slightly out of our local area. My crewmate and I had another member of staff with us this day that were just finishing up their last year before qualifying as a paramedic.

We often have students accompany us on the vehicles as well as other members of staff who are doing an internal route through the service to achieve their hours to register as a paramedic.

A call came through about a woman that was being aggressive to their carer, who was finding it difficult to deal with her, had called 999. With most mental health cases we often get extra information that helps us assess the job before attending. As we discussed the job an update appeared on the computer and said, "Site: Approach With Caution".

Intrigued by the update we called the control room to ask for more information about the 'flagged-up' message. They told us that there were no other details. This was a cause for concern as usually there is more information to help us before we attend.

We arrived at the job and parked to the rear of the property that was in a block of flats. Around the estate there were many broken fence panels and lots of graffiti on the walls. These are all the things that make you more cautious of your surroundings.

Kids were playing out on bikes and others were kicking a ball about the street. It was great to see them out playing. These were the kind of kids that would often wave to us as we drove past with the lights and siren activated.

We approached the door and pressed the buzzer, there was no answer so we pressed again. After three or four attempts a lady stuck her head out of a first-floor window and asked if we would be like to be let in. She was not the patient but a neighbour.

We finally gained entry to the block and gradually made our way up the stairs. Then discovered that the address was on the top floor! I knocked on the door and after a few minutes heard someone coming to the door. There was the sound of a chain and bolt being drawn back and the door suddenly opened.

A lady stood square in the doorway and asked us why we were there. Half of her head was shaved and wore a star printed onesie that had several holes in it.

I looking back on this now, I'm not sure why I didn't notice the strange look on her face sooner but her expression indicated that something was not quite right about the situation.

My crewmate was standing closest to the door, talking to the patient, our student was in the middle and I was at the rear carrying all the equipment. We were invited inside and entered a square lobby that led on to an open plan lounge. Adjacent doors led off to a kitchen and bedroom.

As we entered the lounge there was a three-seater sofa facing away from us and towards a matching sofa, under a window, on the other side of the room which faced in our direction.

The lady walked into the lounge and laid herself across the sofa in front of us. She started to raise her voice and became more and more agitated and about us being there. My crewmate walked around the sofa to try and strike up a conversation that might help calm her down.

I tried to talk to her as well but my attempts had no effect at all. She appeared to have a dislike towards men. Maybe this was due to a bad experience with medical workers in the past or something unrelated in her personal life. The bottom line is we shall never know.

I began to get the paperwork out of the kit bag. I thought it might be better if I stopped talking and fill out the paperwork to save some time.

There are sometimes in your life when someone says something to you that you're not quite sure you've heard properly. For a brief moment you think to yourself, "What did they say?" You probably heard it correctly but can't quite believe it or in disbelief as to what had been said.

I had just started the paperwork when our student approached and whispered to me something that will haunt me for a very long time. She lent in and whispered, "She has a gun". There was an immediate silence in the room and a very long pause. I stopped what I was doing and tried to mentally digest what had just been said.

Did I hear correctly? Did she just say what I thought she did? I played it over and over quickly in my mind but it was true, she did say exactly what I thought I had heard. Words that gave me a shiver and froze my feet to the floor where you stood.

I whispered back and asked where it was and was it a real gun? Asking that question seemed like such a stupid question, for it had to be treated as real until we knew different.

The student said that it was on the floor in front of the patient next to the chair. My crewmate who had walked around the sofa, had spotted it and decided to put the defibrillator on top of the gun to hide it from view.

Looking back on it now, I wondered why she did not just retreat when she saw the gun, make excuses to leave and for us to get to immediate safety.

I had no idea that the patient heard my whispered conversation. All of a sudden she rolled off the sofa and reached for the gun that was on the floor. She quickly panned around in my direction, followed by the sound of a preliminary click from the gun that sounded like it was loaded ready to use. The barrel was five feet away pointing straight at my head. She suddenly screamed at me and shouted, "You're not taking my fucking gun". I tried to react quickly but my feet had frozen rendering me unable to move or do anything.

You often hear, in situations like this, people saying that they see their life flashing in front of them. Seeing all manner of things, some can be random, others being personal to them. I had images of my family. My son was only two at the time, so young. This current situation made me think that I may not get to see any of them again.

At times like this your life gets put into a certain perspective. It makes you realise how you can go about your daily job and how things can change in an instant.

I wasn't sure what to do first. My instinct was to jump out of the way but also a part of me wanted to grab my crewmate or even to get hold of the gun. Fight or flight is a scary thing, a body's natural response to a stressful or dangerous situation.

Not being in a situation like this before, I had no idea what to do, or what would be the safest option without any of us being hurt. The first thing that I could think to do was to grab the arm of the student and say that we needed to get out of the door.

My other crewmate had already committed themselves to the other side of the room. There was no way that I would be able to get to them in time without myself or them being shot. The sofa was a physical barrier, not only for me but for them to get out quickly and get to safety.

I hit my panic button and shouted, "Put the gun down, the patient has a gun".

The student and I managed to get to the front door, opened it and got onto the landing. At this point the student screamed the name of our crewmate who was still inside. We could hear her saying to the patient, "I'm leaving, I'm leaving" and within moments the door opened – a further amount of fear shook through me as we didn't know if it was the patient on the other side with a gun in hand. Fortunately it was my crewmate, she managed to get out and within seconds we made our way down the stairs as quick as we could and exited the door at the bottom. The ambulance was only a short distance away and at the time it seemed the safest place for us to retreat to.

We sat there for the next few moments and reflected on what had just happened. We had no idea where the patient was, did they follow us down the stairs? It was important to get ourselves together mentally as well as physically. We had to try and think clearly as all of our lives, at this moment, depended on it.

We called the control room to tell them what had taken place. Since I'd hit the panic button they had not called us throughout the episode but they had been listening to what had taken place and that crucial information would be relayed onto the police.

We had been out of the property approximately three or four minutes when the controller on the radio stated that a manager was on route followed by the HART team who assist in difficult situations.

The HART team had been formed following a series of terror incidents and was the government's multi-agency approach to responding more effectively to serious incidents.

Within fifteen minutes a manager arrived and began to assess the scene. They reported back to the control room with the relevant information as to what had taken place.

Alongside our day-to-day roles in the service, there are also opportunities to offer assistance in other areas. The service regularly assists with the AIT team (Ambulance Intervention Team) and these members of staff are trained to stabilise and remove an injured patient back to safety from a hostile area.

I had undergone my training in this area around a year beforehand and, although I had no control over what had already taken place, it suddenly occurred to me that I could use elements of this training to help with information regarding the property and the patient.

I began to draw a floor plan of the property on the whiteboard in the ambulance. This was with the view of explaining the layout of the rooms, where the patient and last known position of the gun were positioned in the property. It was also important to explain the number of entrances and exits. The police and HART team would depend on this knowledge to execute a safe entry to the property.

Some ten minutes later the HART team arrived, we got asked to move the ambulance up the road to a safer location which was also a rendezvous with the police for a briefing. We began to explain everything again as well as walking them through the layout of the property. They were just getting ready to meet with the police when a call came over the radio to explain that the patient was now in custody. An immediate sense of relief was felt throughout the ambulance. We began to relax when we were asked by the police to bring the ambulance back round to the property.

It had occurred to us at this point that the police had only been on scene for a matter of moments after we had left, a further indicator as to how quickly things had been moving.

As we slowed the ambulance down we saw the police walking the patient out of the property in cuffs. It was the first time we had seen her since leaving and I noticed that her face still displayed that complete look of detachment from reality. She was seated in the rear of the ambulance and, despite everything that had taken place, still required an assessment to see if she was alright.

At that point, time seemed to have changed for me. It was as though I was behind by a few minutes as events unfolded and I was slowly catching up.

The patient was assessed by one of the HART team paramedics. It was safer for us to remain out of view of the patient herself. The news of her being required to attend hospital resonated with us. We were the only ambulance at the scene and the fact was that we were going to have to take her with the police escort.

A HART paramedic, along with the police, travelled in the back for the short distance to the local hospital. A five-minute trip seemed like a lot longer but we soon arrived to drop the patient off.

We all sat there collecting our thoughts as the patient was escorted into the hospital. Soon after we were told that we were 'good to go' and the job was brought to a close. We got back into the vehicle and called the control room to advise them that the job had been concluded.

We returned back to our local station but there was nobody about, not even a manager, so we sat and had a cup of tea discussing the job. The first thing that stood out was all of the things that went wrong, the things that essentially could have put us in further danger.

Although we can pull any job apart, we will all have a point of view. Mine was that I could not understand why my colleague had committed themselves, after seeing the gun, in entering the lounge and to engage with the patient.

There is no doubt that it had been a difficult job but one we can all learn from no matter what your point of view. Two hours had past while we chatted but it didn't seem to take that long. At one point in my reality there had been a kind of time lag but now time was moving quicker than ever. The speed of time doesn't change of course but it just showed me how much you can think about things after they have taken place.

I needed to speak to someone else about the job so decided to call a manager. He told me that he had heard about the job but could not be there straight away as he was just finishing up on another assignment. After about thirty minutes he finally arrived. We explained about the job we had just attended and that no debrief had taken place. My two crewmates explained that they wished to stand down the remainder of the shift. There were only a few hours left so seemed the best course of action.

The manager on duty was also in fact my line manager. I also explained that I wished to return home, so we all began to collect our things and finish for the day. With the day brought to a close, the reflection of what had taken place still played on my mind as I drove the twenty-minute journey back home.

I sat in the car outside my house trying to figure out how I was going to explain to my family what had taken place at work that day. You leave your home every day and think that you will be helping to make a difference to people's lives and not staring down the barrel of a gun!

Explaining things was no easy task. Just attempting to relay the story had a harsh impact on the listener who was trying to digest the words. That evening seemed to go slowly, the polar opposite of how fast the day had passed earlier, although both irregular passages of time had their own effect on you in a different kind of way.

I didn't sleep much that night – my brain was so occupied. I had trouble in shutting down with all the unanswered questions my mind had racked up since the incident took place.

Night times were definitely the worst. The days that followed the incident almost made time stand still and my head appeared to be caught in a loop. It was really hard to get to sleep. Countless times I would wake up in the middle of the night with an image etched into my mind of the gun pointing at my head. It's accurate to say that nobody will ever know the true fear of a situation until you're presented with it. Some people might think, "But you are fine, get over it", others might equally know they would feel the same as me or worse.

I was due on duty the next day as well as the day after but it hadn't even occurred to me to see how I felt. I tried to keep myself busy and getting 'back on the horse' seemed like a good idea.

I was expecting some engagement from management but nothing had been said but assumed it would probably take a while before I heard anything from them. It was around four days after the incident, when I was at home on a rest day, when something just clicked in my mind – enough was enough, I called senior management.

I explained everything and that I was unhappy with how the lacking the aftercare was considering what had happened. We were still unsure if the gun itself was real, let alone what the sentence was going to be.

I decided to take some time off. Around a week had passed and, in that time, I went to give a statement to the police with what had happened. The officer began to tell me something I could not comprehend. He went on to explain that the Crown Prosecution Service had made a decision, because the patient had been suffering from poor mental health, at the time of the incident, they deemed her not capable of standing trial.

It was right after this we discovered that the gun, although very realistic, was a replica. I immediately began to think just how flawed the legal system is, not only was she not being charged regarding the weapon, and threatening us with it, the whole incident was swayed towards a mental health problem.

After this we heard no more about it, although in my mind the incident itself has never gone away. Now when I attend a patient that has a poor mental health condition, and I know there could be a possible risk attached to it, I stop and question every element of it. Incidents such as these can, within moments, bring visions of the previous job flooding back. This can be an awful feeling as you never know who has called 999 and if they are in desperate need of our help.

For the most we have to take it all in our stride, job after job we just get on with it. However, we also know that the uniform we wear is not a shield or bulletproof vest, all we have is the scars from previous jobs to help protect us as we go on to the next.

Everything you want is on the other side of fear.

Jack Canfield

8 | Anguish and Apparition

HAVE YOU EVER had an experience you can't explain? An experience so strange that it leaves you questioning what took place even though your adamant of what you've just seen.

In the service we see and experience many unusual things, some more strange than the next, but I suppose, the fact that we are in and around death it is more likely that odd things might happen to us at some point.

I have always believed that there is something after we pass away, what it is, and where we go, nobody will truly know until the time comes. There are also many sceptics in the service, some just brush off what they have experienced, maintaining that they didn't really see what just took place in front of them.

I have worked with some people that say, 'seeing is believing'. They too believe that there must be something, but just want that confirmation.

Over the years I have often visited places such as care homes and felt as if I wasn't alone – that eerie sense as if I was being watched. It is a feeling that you don't forget, one that leaves you questioning yourself somewhat.

It was a bright sunny day and I was roughly half way through my shift when we were assigned a call for a possible hanging. I have attended a few hangings over the years. As much as they are the same in nature, they have always been different in circumstance. By this I mean, the method of how this is carried out, such as types of equipment used, rope, wire, all manner of objects.

The call itself was five miles away. This may not seem far but in reality it can take some time to cover this amount of ground depending on traffic and road conditions.

We went as fast as we could and were advised by control that the police were ahead of us and would be first on the scene. When it comes to suicide there are a few things that you mentally learn to take into account when attending this kind of job.

The first thing is that we never know what has driven the patient to do what they've done. Everyone has a story – it is not fair for anyone to judge or even form an opinion to what has taken place in the hours that led up to the event itself.

You can walk into a patient's home and see all manner of things, empty bottles, cans, medication packets, this does not mean that these were consumed today or even the day before. Some people choose to live in an untidy environment, this is just an everyday part of their life due physical or mental health problems but, on the face of it, one could assume it all took place over recent hours or days.

We arrived at the property to discover two police cars parked with their blue lights still flashing. This in itself shows the speed they must have gone, to get to the patient in time, in order to attempt to save their life.

The house itself was the type that I like to call a 'back-back house', they are the design that has no rear garden and one house backs on to another and only having a front garden.

I got to the front gate and put my hand out to open it so that we could gain entry. It was then I observed a little girl playing with her toys on the ground, she couldn't of been any more than 6 or 7 years of age.

Knowing how quickly I needed to get into the house, I asked the little girl if she could move back so that we could get past her to make our way inside.

As this was said, she stood up and ran inside the property with us coming in behind her. We stepped inside and saw her run to the end of the hallway and off to the right.

As we got to the hallway a police officer stepped out into the hall and directed us to the patient. My first observation was the sense of calm on the officer's face. Normally in a situation where there is a medical emergency you would detect a sense of urgency, this however was not the case here.

He explained, that when they arrived they discovered the patient was just sitting on the sofa, with the rope around his neck, contemplating ending his life.

This was a huge relief for us, not only was the patient safe, it meant that despite everything, that may or may not have led to this, we could possibly get them some help. We managed to obtain vital observations and the patient at this point had also agreed to come to hospital. It was nice to see a positive outcome for such a job. In some cases we don't always get to the patient in time, today was a good example of multi-agencies working together to preserve life.

As we were getting ready to leave, the wife entered the room. I used this opportunity to request her assistance and she made it very clear that she wished to come with the patient to hospital.
I asked her if she could pack the patient a bag for the usual necessities that she thinks he may require. We began to get into a conversation.

This is when I said something to her that her response made me turn cold and felt my heart pound as a result.

I said, "If she was travelling with us, did she want to sort out someone to come and sit with her daughter." She was walking across the room as I was putting this to her, she stopped instantly and responded, "What did you just say?". Again I repeated what I had just said.

She said to me, "What gives you the idea that we have a daughter? – That is what this is all about". I asked her what she meant by, 'what this was all about', she replied and said that three years ago their daughter had become really ill and sadly passed away.

I didn't know what to say but yet she asked me again what I meant by my comment. I replied, "That when I was in the lounge, I saw photos on the wall, as well as other areas, all family photos with yourself, the patient, and a young girl".

I was trying to think on my feet, whilst still trying to understand what I had seen a short while before. She went on to explain that they no longer have a daughter as she had passed away a few years ago and that her partner had never got over it.

A feeling of cold came over me and the hairs on the back of my neck and arms stood up. Who was that I had seen outside and had run into the house? I needed to satisfy my own curiosity so went back into the lounge. I instantly was met by the photos that covered different areas of the walls, all showing a loving family home.

It was her, the girl we had seen in the garden, I must have looked five or six times, all with the intention of correcting myself as to the fact it must have been a mistake. My crewmate looked to me, he could see the shocked look on my face. I needed to understand what had just taken place in the other room.

I know he witnessed what I did in the front garden, he too was entering the gate the same time I had, this said I needed to know for sure.

We began to make our way off to hospital. Being in so much shock and disbelief my crewmate attended in the back with the patient for the journey. We got to A&E where we handed over to the nurse and said our goodbyes.

Upon returning to the vehicle, my crewmate said to me, "What on earth is wrong, you look really unwell?". I began asking them to talk me through what they observed about the job from when we arrived at the scene. I wanted that clarity, just something to reaffirm the fact I wasn't going mad and that what we had seen really took place.

We ran through the job, it was confirmed – he had seen the same thing!

I went on to explain what the partner had said to me... the fact that she had said the daughter had passed away, along with me mentioning about some childcare whilst we went to hospital.

You could feel an overwhelming sense of shock in the vehicle, we were trying to comprehend what had just taken place. We went over the job so many times to try and understand what we had both seen. I even went as far as asking the police if they had checked every room before leaving, just to make sure there was no children, this was also from a safeguarding standpoint due to the nature of the call.

The police had stated that all rooms were clear, they were happy to follow us to the hospital to just finalise some paperwork. This was the last bit of clarity that we needed. We both looked at each other in such disbelief that, still to this day, I still question the job.

Was the little girl just making her presence known to comfort and help her father? Were we being shown the way to her father to give him the required help he needed?

I don't think we will ever find out why, nor do I think I will ever fully come to terms with what I had seen. Looking back, I do think it was nice that she had made her presence known, considering the amount of sorrow that was in the home.

In the hours that followed the handover to the staff at hospital, this is one incident that really did leave us scratching our heads.

The spiritual journey is the unlearning of fear and prejudices and the acceptance of love back in our hearts.

Marianne Williamson

9 | No Fixed Abode

W E ENCOUNTER PEOPLE from all walks of life and it becomes very much a part of our job to come across members of the homeless community. Some may be sitting in a doorway, some busking with a guitar, or seeing some arrested for shoplifting in sheer desperation in a bid for food.

Within the first few months of being in the service, it became very apparent that we were seeing a rise in the number of patients that were of 'no fixed abode', some out of choice, some due to a relationship break-down, as well as some that have lost everything through losing their job.

The first thing that struck me, was the terminology that is used by modern society to describe this community. Terms such as, 'vagrant', 'down and out', 'hobo', 'tramp', all these highlights how detached we have become towards people who are less fortunate than ourselves.

You will often see some begging for money, some who look like they have also not eaten in days. When asked how often people will give them money, most will say not often, this is with an apparent concern that it will be spent on drink or drugs, or even both.

In the service it is not uncommon to get a call for an overdose such as a man or woman who is completely unresponsive with tell-tale track marks on their arms or legs. This is the reality of the lengths some people go to when it comes to coping with everyday life.

On occasion you can often get into conversation with a homeless person whilst treating them. Such as asking the last time they ate, or had a hot drink would usually get them talking and from time-time, some would open up and tell you their story – the journey that led them to end up where they are today. Gambling, drug misuse, even a breakdown in the marriage can result in a husband or wife to end up out on the street.

It is here where people end up mixing in certain circles, Circles that can be kind of a roulette wheel when it comes to who tries to befriend you. From here it doesn't take long for drink or drugs to enter the mix, which later leads on to an addiction that needs to be fed.

When I heard my first few stories, it struck me that some of these homeless people were very well educated and even well-to-do individuals. They were down on their luck with nowhere to turn.

For us, hospital was the only place to go, there was no immediate resource to step in and wave a magic wand. Within a short while I was introduced to a man who worked at a local shelter, he volunteered there, provided hot food, along with donations of clothing from time to time. He told me about the great efforts that were provided, the work that went into it, along with their mission to provide a better place for everyone.

I was really taken aback with all the effort that had gone into this venture, all off of their own backs – they did not seek for glory, just wanted to help. How had I not heard of this before? After some time, I began to have more and more dealings with the shelter in the area. The most significant thing was that not all of the patients we go to at the shelter require hospital treatment.

Following a few meetings, I was privileged to go and assist at the shelter, this would sometimes consist of looking at the sores on people's feet, giving talks and general medical advice.

It didn't take long to discover that some of these people had either been struck off by their GP or had even given up on the GP altogether. I tried to be objective and became very conscious of the fact that there may be a different side to every story told. Some may have declined help, or not attended an appointment, or even not received letters due to being of no fixed abode.

I started to catalogue all the things that were coming up time and time again. There appeared to be a clear breakdown in communication. No link that bridged the gap between discharge of care and the patient being met with an alternative pathway.

In winter the temperature can drop to below freezing so it was not an uncommon sight to discover patients that had died as a result of hypothermia.

There needed to be more, something to prevent the cycle of events that seemed to be happening over and over again. I began to sit in on meetings with the local authority and the local homeless charities that were trying to make a difference.

It was then that I tried to formulate a plan. I wasn't even sure if it would work but had to try anyway. My goal was to step in and attempt to provide an alternative solution to the ever-evolving problem the community was facing.

The first thing that I noticed was, by attending the shelter every Wednesday, it provided a familiar face, one that encouraged people to speak up, to actually say how well they were doing or problems such as barriers that they had been met with.

As much as the local authority was doing its best, the biggest problem was that they relied on the information of external agencies as to where these individuals were in terms of housing and care.

As I was already working within the medical service, I found I was in an advantageous position, one in which enabled me to see both sides of the fence. I heard accounts of the homeless situation from both patient and agency.

It soon dawned on me that a lot of what the patients were telling me was not the same as the agencies were stating in the monthly meeting. Some crucial information was getting lost along the way.

I spoke to my bosses and looked into the possibility of using a community hall, one in which that could provide a multi-agency get-together. This would allow the homeless community to have a place to meet with each agency and then the agencies could discuss the problems patients were having. This was with a view to developing stronger communication, a better transition of care, as well as trust between the community and us.

Following several emails, I eventually got to meet with other agencies, to propose my plans, to let people see my vision and, as a service, what we encounter day-to-day on the frontline.

The reception was fantastic. Coming up with a name for this new service took weeks but I finally settled on one after feedback from friends. It was that day I launched 'The Community Impact Scheme' – a day where I was determined to make a difference.

I arranged a meeting again with several of the agencies to discuss our plans, reservations, along with a projection for the future and a full prospectus was formulated. Now it was time for me to go back to my bosses and compare various angles that really affect us every day as a service.

One of the biggest challenges the hospitals have faced, over the last few decades, is the increased demand for immediate medical treatment for what are often minor conditions. This has had a huge impact on the already stretched resources of the NHS. Although we need to keep homeless people safe and well it has become a common occurrence that hospitals are the only option for them with nowhere else to go – a place that is safe, so they are not left on the streets, but not ideal.

I had several discussions with shelters and other services to see what our options were to help ease this situation. Their main concern was that there were so many people that attended the shelter and that they did not have the expertise or time to know who were sick and required treatment. It was then that I came up with a solution, one that suited both parties and would prove to have an appropriate outcome.

It had also been discussed that the shelters had limited funds and were also stretched when it came to mouths to feed – everything they achieved was due to the kindness of people's donations. The shelter went on to say that they did a sponsored sleep-out every year and needed to raise money fast.
The thought of them struggling financially encouraged me to get sponsored and join the volunteers for a night's sleep-out to see what it would be like to spend a night on the streets.

I created a fundraising page with GoFundMe to help raise money for the shelter – the response was phenomenal. We raised a total of £3,877 in just one week, a remarkable step in supporting the struggling volunteers in their continuing mission to further help the homeless.

The conditions on that night were freezing but it gave me a good understanding of what the homeless community have to face on a daily basis. For us it was just for 12 hours but for them it is a regular occurrence that forms part of their everyday life. I learnt a lot from that night – the biggest thing was to try and appreciate every day, as all of us are just three pay cheques away from potentially being homeless.

```
A MILE IN HER SHOES EVENT &          0025
COMMUNITY IMPACT SCHEME
                            DATE 20.12.19
PAY TO THE
ORDER OF  Three  Thousand   Eight   £ 3,877
Hundred  And  Seventy  Seven
                                    POUNDS
MEMO
                           AUTHORIZED SIGNATURE
⑈789123456⑈ 123789456123⑈ 0025
```

After the fundraising we agreed that we would stop by the shelter, whilst on duty, to check if there were any immediate medical concerns that we could see to then and there. This was also followed up by the shelter reserving two bed spaces that the ambulance service could use for the homeless. They knew we would only be in touch with them if our patient did not require hospital admittance and that we would have medically cleared the patient before we dropped them off to the shelter. This new procedure turned out to save fourteen bed spaces at the hospital per week. This may not seem a lot but, in reality, it was a huge saving.

A rapport was beginning to build up between the crews and the homeless and we were developing a good relationship with them. The project was beginning to gain traction and it became a win-win situation all round.

After a few weeks we began to get some really positive feedback from the crews. We were finally getting a more appropriate outcome for our patients and it felt really good. That warm feeling you get, when you feel you have made a difference, is one you do not forget.

I began to promote a second-hand clothing project at the station. The plan was to donate any old clothing that could be dropped off and used by the shelter which they would then hand out after the meal on a

Wednesday. Within a short while the clothes started coming in, bag after bag, for us to drop off.

Clothing that would otherwise be sitting in the wardrobe or chest of draws was going to good use. On the whole, the overall impact, of working together, had been amazing. By simple word of mouth the project had provided some better care that this community really deserved.

It was around eight months later, when I was finishing my lunch, that my phone notified me that I had an email. It was from the office of the chief executives. I was really puzzled, why was I getting this kind of email? I had

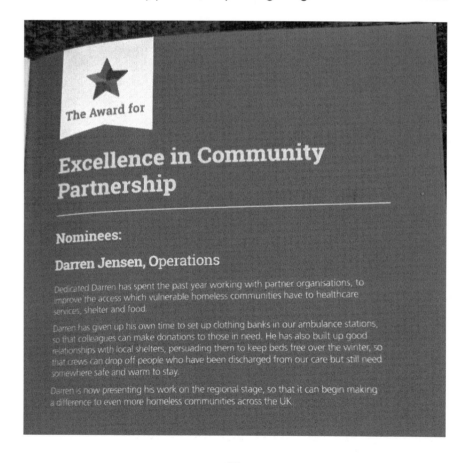

The Award for

Excellence in Community Partnership

Nominees:

Darren Jensen, Operations

Dedicated Darren has spent the past year working with partner organisations, to improve the access which vulnerable homeless communities have to healthcare services, shelter and food.

Darren has given up his own time to set up clothing banks in our ambulance stations, so that colleagues can make donations to those in need. He has also built up good relationships with local shelters, persuading them to keep beds free over the winter, so that crews can drop off people who have been discharged from our care but still need somewhere safe and warm to stay.

Darren is now presenting his work on the regional stage, so that it can begin making a difference to even more homeless communities across the UK.

been nominated and shortlisted for an 'Excellence in Community Partnership' award. My chin hit the floor. I began to read on... The email went on to say that, following the extensive work that has been put into improving the local community, the project has been recognised for an award. I was ecstatic, I really could not believe it. I had not started the project with the view of getting praise or an award but the thought of being recognised, for the work I'd done, was really nice.

A few months later I received an email with details of the awards evening. The date was not far away and came around really quickly. I was given the day off work to help me prepare for the evening. I was excited but I knew there were many other people who were just as deserving as I was for their contributions to the community.

The evening started with a nice meal and drinks and then led on to the names being called for the various different award categories. All the nominees were amazing and this just confirmed to me the great team of colleagues that I worked with on a daily basis.

As I was following the nominations in the programme booklet, it eventually came around to the Community Partnership Award. My hands began to sweat with anticipation. The details of each nominee were read aloud for all to hear, then the details of my project were read out. At this point there was a long pause that seemed to last forever – then I heard my name called. There were spontaneous shouts of excitement from everyone at the table that gave me a great sense of joy and pleasure.

It took a few moments but finally I made my way to the stage to receive my award which was a glass trophy with my name etched in it. I picked it up and had my photo taken. The feel of it in my hands instantly made me look back at how better things had become.

It wasn't long before I went back to my normal shifts and going about my day attending my patients.

My crewmate and I were sitting on a standby point waiting for the next job to come through when, all of a sudden, my phone rang. It was a member of senior management who explained that, following the award ceremony, my name had been put forward to attend a further ceremony. I had to ask them to repeat what they had said and it took me a moment for the penny to drop. They told me I had been nominated to attend the 'Queens Royal Garden Party' on behalf of the trust. I sat there in complete disbelief. Another positive thing, in my life, that I had to let sink in.

Following this nomination Covid-19, unfortunately, had an impact on things being able to take place. However, ceremony or not, just the thought of it and to see my name on the piece of paper was absolutely amazing.

Your past is just a story. And once you realize this it has no power over you.

Chuck Palahniuk

From: – – – –
Sent: 10 February 2020 | 14:54
To: – – – –
Subject: Action: Royal Garden Party Allocation - replies by *10 Feb*
Importance: High

Good afternoon.

Please see below invitation to the Royal Garden Party.

Darren Jenson and – – – – have been nominated to attend – please could you call Darren and – – – – to congratulate them on the nomination.

Please could you forward their addresses for me to complete the relevant paperwork – I have to submit this by COP today.

Thanks

– – – –

From: RGP
Sent: 10 January 2020 | 17:04
To: – – – –
Subject: Action: Royal Garden Party Allocation - replies by 29th Jan

For the attention of the Chief Executive

Dear: Chief Executive,

I am writing to inform you that The Queen will hold three Royal Garden Parties at Buckingham Palace in 2020 on Tuesday 12th May, Tuesday 19th May and Wednesday 27th May 2020.

I am pleased to offer your organisation a total allocation of 2 places as below:

10 | Man Down

MANY OF US can go throughout our lives with nothing out of the ordinary ever taking place but sometimes we can equally overlook things that are right in front of us.

The emergency services are a profession that can be, at times, very stressful. Whether it's the police, fire or ambulance service, we all have expectations, and aspirations for our future. From the outset we have undergone intensive study and training to accomplish our goals, further our career and progress to bigger and better things.

One thing that really struck me, when I joined the service, was the wide difference in everybody's background. Some finished their education with good grades and qualifications while others left school with nothing whatsoever. My grades were not fantastic when I left school but I wanted to have the best possible chance to achieve my dreams, in whatever career I set my sights on, in the future.

We get to know our colleagues, in the service, very well and on average we spend more time with them than we do at home. This gives us the opportunity to have open and honest discussions on most days. We will often chat about our children growing up, the day-day stresses of life in general and the state of our mental health.

One particular case that comes to mind was a colleague who started the service the same time as I did who had dyslexia. He was a bit younger than myself but I could see that his outlook on life was very much similar to mine in terms of his career path.

There had been a lot of information going around about upcoming courses. One of these was designed to help staff to progress to the next level of clinical qualification to become a paramedic.

The advert that went out was fantastic, it outlined that staff could apply no matter what their existing grades were. The expectation was that there were two separate courses to run, both of which to achieve the same outcome, but entry assessments were to take on board the different learning strengths of each applicant.

The staff were ecstatic, many expressed an interest and applied for the course. A short list of people was drawn up as there were limited spaces available for the upcoming intake. It was some time before people heard back about their applications. Before long this particular member of staff got an email to say that he had been successful in making the shortlist. He then had to attend the university and undertake an assessment in English as well as maths, along with a face-face interview.

He was very apprehensive waiting for the email response.
The email finally came through and said that he had been successful and a forthcoming date was given to attend the University for the next steps that had to take place.

I remember how I felt when my assessment took place, clammy hands, stomach churning and all the other nervous reactions that you might expect. He explained to me that it all appeared to be a straight forward assessment at first, although things quickly changed when they said that they don't make allowances for dyslexia. I could see his disappointment on hearing this. All the hard work and effort, he had put into the day, now felt like it was in vain. Despite this he had given it his best shot, although he experienced horrific anxiety waiting for the results that were due later that day.

It's scary to think that all your dreams are in the hands of someone else. Am I good enough? Can I do it? Sometimes we might see ourselves, in the future, where a turn of events has placed us in a positive position – his now relied on the outcome of an email.

It was a long time waiting for an answer. He told me that it was almost as if time had stood still. His email alert went off – it was from the university with the outcome of the assessment – he had failed. The feedback was that he had been unsuccessful due to his spelling and grammar, and slightly on the maths paper.

His dreams were shattered even though he had been open and transparent about his additional learning needs beforehand. He had been on a huge high only a few weeks before, but now having been slammed down to earth, it was a hard thing to come to terms with.

It was a few days before I spoke to him again, and what would have been a normal chat, didn't seem the same this time. I'm sure we can all think of a conversation we've had in the past with someone where you can see that they're looking at you but not taking in a single bit of what is said.

The first big change was his lack of engagement with his peers. Conversation with him did not seem the same as they had been before. It was only a short while after this that I was told he was not sleeping well or eating and drinking properly. These were all indicators that depression was starting to unfold. One by one these traits caused him more and more emotional and physical barriers. What was once a laughing and joking kind of guy was now a very different person.

I decided to pull him to one side and ask how he was feeling. He didn't need to even open his mouth for me to understand – it was clearly visible just by the look on his face. We had a chat about the events that had taken place. He told me that, from the outset, it had been made clear to him that, to even get on the course in the first place, his academic struggles would have been taken into consideration.

It was very clear that there had not been enough support given, along with a very evident breakdown in communication between the employer and the university itself. You would like to think, that in circumstances such as these, provisions would have been put in place to more easily accommodate people with dyslexia. In this modern day and age it is known that more and more people have additional educational requirements.

Over the years there have been some amazing people with great minds that have struggled with dyslexia such as Steven Spielberg, Winston Churchill and Thomas Edison but they have all gone on to achieve great things and make their mark on the world.

This in itself just goes to show that setbacks of this nature really should not happen in today's age as there are so many more resources available than there were. To be dropped at the first obstacle really isn't right. It was difficult to explain to my friend that this setback was not necessarily the end and that there will be other opportunities in the future. In some ways it was difficult to say this to him as I had already passed my assessments and was on the course.

He was invited back for another assessment and, following a chat with the university, he was advised that he would only have to sit the elements that he had failed. This had been arranged by the head of the course, someone in a position of authority who had recognised it had only been a marginal failure.

Speaking to him a few days later it was like a huge weight had been lifted from his shoulders – a second ray of hope, to get on the course, was now in sight.

It had not been clear if the university themselves were going to recognise his educational setback, or if they were going offer any addition support. The only thing that they had made clear was that he only had to marginally improve in the one failed elements.

Although the employer was also aware of their decision, they said that this just felt like a passive acknowledgement and that nothing was being done or put into place. All this just contributed to an overwhelming anxiety for the road ahead.

I did not see him for about a week although we did stay in touch by phone, a kind of remote support as and when needed on days that he felt low.

The conversations that did follow were all really positive and he explained that he had being paying for private lessons to help with passing his upcoming assessment. His clear passion and determination were amazing, it just told me that nothing was going to prevent him from achieving his dream.

Things settled down somewhat and it was as though life had returned to normal and that nothing had ever happened. This was until a few weeks later when I received a message from him to say that today was the day of his second attempt.

The assessment would take place at around 10am and I was really rooting for him as the amount of hard work he had done was incredible. It must have been around one o'clock in the afternoon that my phone rang and, looking at the screen, I could see it was him calling. I had my fingers crossed as I answered the call. There was a long pause before I asked him how he got on.

Have you ever had that feeling when you know that something isn't quite right? Well, this was one of those occasions. The details he gave me in the call even made me upset. He explained that he arrived all set to be tested on just the final elements that had been requested. When he spoke to a member of the university faculty, and told them he had already passed the interview along with other elements of the assessment, they explained that he still had to sit the whole assessment and every element all over again.

To say that I was heartbroken for him was an understatement. Not only was he not advised of this beforehand and did not have the chance to prepare, he had not dressed appropriately for a second interview. He explained that he gave it another go regardless. With these assessments you have to achieve a set overall level to pass and what with him not being dressed appropriately would go against his overall score. This contributed to a complete change in his mind set and he was not being able to think clearly due to anxiety.

I asked him what was said on the day. They told him it was not university policy to change the rules and that there were no exceptions – even though something different had been arranged beforehand. Understandably the impact of what had taken place had an overwhelming effect on his confidence and his mental health as a whole.

Within moments you could just sense, in his voice, that he was in a very bad place. He said that he was alright but the tone of the voice told a very different story. In the days that followed he became withdrawn and didn't talk much or participate in anything.

Throughout this whole ordeal I had a few conversations with his partner. It was very evident how much of a support she had been to him. She stood strong even when he was at a huge low no matter how tough it got. She told me he was in a very dark place.

It didn't matter what was said to him from this point on. It was as if he had made his mind up about himself, his life and the future. I suppose once you're in that place it is like a form of tunnel vision that prevents you seeing any positive s or alternative solutions.

I kept asking myself if I could have done more? What had I missed? Was there an angle that I could have approached from a different direction? All I could think of was that our employer should have stepped in sooner and that maybe management could have been an advocate for him at each step.

I contacted management and explained my concerns. He was invited to a meeting to look at the whole situation. In the meantime, the training and education department did have discussions with him and said that, due to the number of attempts he'd made at the assessment, there was nothing that they could do but would try an attempt at changing their decision.

With his mental health the way it was, it was clear that this was not an option for him to sit a further test at the moment. Things needed to change because the process, that had been followed, was not fair at all. If the policy was that the whole assessment had to be sat again then there was a clear breaking of the rules when he had been advised to only sit a small element.

A meeting with senior management had concluded that there was nothing more they could do on a local level and that all options, that were at their disposal, had been exhausted, with this said he felt that it was a very passive response, in balance, not only to him as an employee but also to someone's future.

What really struck me was the impact poor mental health has on someone. Not only does it hit them regarding the situation that has caused it, it also hits hard in every other element of their life such as in general relationships and at home as well.

Becoming distant, withdrawn, snappy was an all too familiar appearance, all of which had become worse by the day.

I wasn't sure which direction the whole ordeal was going to take. All I did know was that someone needed to step in and try and cushion the fall so to speak. I emailed management and made it very clear that the state of his mental health was in a very dark place and being a work-related issue, someone needed to approach him to help resolve the matter.

Within a few days, things were no better and I decided to give him a call to see if he fancied doing something outside of work. I thought a change of scenery, along with a distraction, may help. The moments that followed made me go cold – words spoken that were never forgotten.

Have you ever got to know someone that well and no matter what they say you can instantly tell if something is not right? This was one of those times. He answered the phone and within seconds I could tell by the tone of his voice something was wrong. There was a vacant response to everything I asked him and it was at this point I asked him, outright, if he was considering doing anything silly? Although I asked the question, I was not actually prepared for him to actually say yes!

He explained to me, that earlier that morning he had been preparing to take his own life later in the evening. He had formulated a plan but would do this away from his family. I felt an instant shiver come over me followed by a huge feeling of sickness in my stomach.

Could I have done more? Had I failed in the support I had given him? What could have driven him to think of this option? No matter how many times I played this over in my mind I realised that, in a situation like this, you can only do so much with the limited resources you have available to you.
I had a very limited window to take action. I asked him to promise that he would not do anything and that I wanted him to see that such a drastic measure would have such a devastating impact on his family and friends.

The conversation lasted around forty-five minutes although it seemed a lot shorter. I suppose that was due to the fear of what could actually take place.

It has been said many times how powerful words are. In the ambulance service 90% of the job is talking to people, helping them feel at ease, calming people at their worst and cheering people up that are also feeling down.

Never in my life did I ever think that I would have to use every inch of my communication skills, to not only keep him calm, but to also talk him down out of the dark suicidal place he was in. What if I said the wrong thing? Could the words that left my mouth drive him that one step further?

My fear built up and overwhelmed me and I knew that once my words had left my mouth I couldn't take them back. We often have to 'think on our feet' and try to find a solution that can not only help but also ensure a long-term support at the same time.

I began emailing senior management whilst I was on the phone. I needed to take some sort of action that could put a halt to the way he had been treated and hope for someone to step in and right a wrong.

I hit the send button and hoped for the best. Within a few moments my phone rang in the background whilst we were on a current call – management were trying to get through to me. Now really wasn't the right time for me to take the call, I needed to make sure that he was ok first.

I asked where he was and he said he was at home with the family. With this said, I needed to make sure his partner was aware of what was taking place. She explained that she was aware and that she is staying with him to ensure he does not go out.

I finished the call and called management back. After explaining everything they said they will get in touch and follow up in person. On one hand it felt too little too late, on the other it needed to happen regardless.

Knowing that these calls had happened I felt a partial weight lift from me although I didn't sleep well that night at all. The next morning arrived and text messages were pinging back and forth. The fact that he was replying was a good thing but it was time for management to step in and do their thing to end this horrible situation.

I later heard that several meetings had taken place and then this was then followed up by a complaint being submitted surrounding the poor treatment and support he had received. The weeks that followed were touch and go.

My phone began to ring and I could see that he was trying to get through. I answered the phone but was nervous to his current state of mind. With this whole situation aside, he is an outstanding clinician, the level of care he gives his patients is second to none and it's awful to think that poor treatment in a health sector can chip away at one's mental health.

He answered and greeted me with a happy tone of voice. He told me that decisive action had been taken regarding his grievance and complaint in the lack of support he had received. The organisation had assigned him a member of staff to ensure he gets on a university course to help him become a paramedic.

Some might say that it really shouldn't have come to this. Some others may see people that consider the options of suicide and attempted suicides as just a cry for help. When you get to know someone well and know their state of mind, it's clear that this is not always the case in some individuals.

The more I reflected on this, the more I come to terms with the fact that there is not enough support for mental health conditions, especially as in the service there is a high percentage of mental trauma that is experienced on a daily basis.

Weeks went by and then I received a message from him telling me he had sat a different assessment, passed and now had a start date for the course. I was over the moon for him. Time passed so quickly and before I knew it, he had already been on the course three months with average assessment scores in the high eighties, this in itself reflected just how deserving he was to be on the course.

There was never any doubt in my mind about his capability as I knew, all along that, he would make an amazing paramedic. It was just a shame about the politics and poor communication he got caught up in. Once he was off and running in the course, all the management told him how pleased they were to see him doing so well.
I was also very pleased that I was able to help with the temporary poor mental health condition of a fellow member of staff.

All in all, a fantastic outcome,

There is nothing impossible to him who will try.

Alexander the Great (attributed)

11 | Deference and Distance

I AM CONFIDENT THAT, when growing up, we can all remember hearing the term, "Respect your elders"? It was a term that resonated a lot with me, that I inevitably passed it on to my own children and per has mentioned it as a passing comment to a child or children that were being disrespectful.

It is crazy to see just how much times have changed over the years. Looking back, though, it was so gradual that people seem to just adapt to the changes as the weeks and months passed by. I can remember when growing up, the stern look that my nan would give one of us if we had been cheeky or disrespectful. There was never the need for a clip around the ear, nor anything else – just the look or raised voice was enough.

Nowadays, there appears to be a clear detachment of young people to the older generation and one hears more and more about it through the media. I can remember reading a few years ago about a group of youths that thought it would be funny to pour flour and eggs over a pensioner who was sat minding their own business. It is saddening to see those kind of incidents happening although we shouldn't tar all youngsters with the same brush.

Recently I was sitting at the ambulance station and was chatting with some colleagues about how things have been recently. The conversation led on to the topic of the rise in appointments for elderly patients. The patient transport division (PTS) have always been busy and, due to a rise in demand, the taking patients to and from appointments had suffered a significant increase.

I love some of the conversations we have had in this division and, as mentioned earlier on, this generation of community have some amazing stories to tell. Some so incredible that they really do make you see how fortunate you are to have the simple home comforts and your family around you.

One of the colleagues went on to tell me about an old lady that they had been to see. The lady had just been waiting for a routine collection following a stay in hospital as a result of falling out of bed and striking her head which caused a laceration.

The lady was 105 years old, lived alone with all her faculties, and was still fully independent. The neighbours realised that something was not right when they discovered that her windows were not open one morning.

The opening of the windows was apparently a regular routine and one that, when you think about it, aided the lady to have the alarm raised by the neighbours to fetch help. This happened as a result of people caring and noticing something out of the ordinary.

It transpired that she had fallen in the night and, unfortunately, had been on the floor throughout the night. This can be dangerous to the elderly and infirm. There could also have been medical complications to the internal organs, should it have been for a longer period of time.

When the patient was returned home my colleague helped her inside and then the most wonderful thing took place. Whilst inside there was a knock at the door and standing at the door was a young girl no more than 10 years old. In her hands she was holding an iPad. She was asked inside and then greeted the old lady in a way that you could clearly see was as a result of a beautiful bond between them both.

The lady said she was the daughter of the neighbour next-door and called in to see her most days. Not only did she love spending time with her elderly friend she also helped her to stay in touch with her son and, that since she'd been doing this, had also helped the old lady to keep in touch with a distant relative. Just the thought of this young person's kindness is enough to make your heart full.

My colleague was understandably taken aback when she found out the lady was 105 years old. She told her she has a son who is 75 years of age and that he lives in San Francisco. He had moved away many years ago and made a life for himself in the States and that he was her only living relative.

She went on to say that her son had a heart condition and had never been able to fly back to the UK to see her. Before the neighbours had moved in next door, that now helped her, she would do her best to talk to her son on the phone or write him a letter. The lady then went on to tell my colleague about the day the little girl, from next-door, turned up with an iPad. She wanted to see if she could go one step further and help the old lady to see her son in person with the use of modern-day technology.

Unbeknown to the lady the family, next-door, had been in touch with the son and began to arrange a way to surprise her with a live video chat. The lady explained that it was one of the most emotional days of her life, she never thought that she would ever be able to see his face again.

All this time she had to make do with photos that she had, as well as some that had been posted over the years. To think that a 10-year-old girl took the initiative to do something so magical, you can only begin to imagine what this gesture has done for the old lady's life. We often hear from time to time the term 'give back', random acts of kindness to put a smile on the faces of the older generation. The maturity in age of this young girl was far in excess of her actual years and whilst she probably didn't fully understand the significance of what the old lady's generation did for our country, she was nevertheless glad to help and support a neighbour in need.

The old lady had many old photos around the home that had been taken back in the day of the Second World War and each of those images unlocked many a story.

It has always struck me how humble the older generation are. To think how little they had in those days – ration books, limited amenities and hand-made clothing that would make-do and be passed down to other members of the family.

The old lady had grown up in a time without the benefit of the Internet. Many people in those days did not have a telephone and the only way to communicate, long-distance, was to send letters back and forth and even then you might have to wait a week or so for a reply. To think that she had been so isolated over the years with no close family. These types of jobs in the service can make things really hit home as to how lucky we really are.

The bond the old lady had with the little girl was so heart-warming that it took you back to your childhood days before modern technology took over. I'm sure we can all relate to the downside of our modern-day devices – how it can separate us from physical social interaction but how we can also take them so much for granted.

Stories such as this old lady and her 10-year-old friend is what we can only hope to see more of. I'm afraid the reality is that these heart-warming tales might become fewer and fewer if we cannot educate the importance of respect towards one another, especially the older generation.

It came to light that, sometime later, some other of my colleagues received calls to a care home for this very same old lady as she understandably needed help and support because of her amazing age. This resulted in her having to go into residential care. She unfortunately had to have another trip to hospital and in the months that followed we were told that she sadly passed away. It is only right to say that, not only did this lovely old lady live to a fantastic age, she was also a shining example of a generation of people that we could all learn a lot from.

It is always a blessing to learn wisdom from the elderly.

Lailah Gifty Akita

12 | Dial Tone

W E ALL HAVE DAYS when things do not necessarily go the way you want them to – misplaced car keys, didn't hear your morning alarm go off. All those things that can put us on the wrong foot for the day. Sometimes the day can change for the worse half way through your shift and you start to hope that it's not going to turn out too badly. The same goes for the staff in the emergency services. No matter if you are a police officer, fire fighter or paramedic – right the way back to the person in the control room in that hour of desperation.

Although these people are presented with difficult situations every day, the effects of what they experience still have a profound impact on these men and women who are the backbone of our community.

It is interesting to see the way we analyse life situations that we're presented with and it is easy to take for granted the jobs that people do. Hopefully we can try to be objective and create a mental picture of what it is like to be in somebody else's shoes for the day. The average person that watches a TV hospital or emergency medical show will only be presented with a highly edited version of what has actually taken place. As exciting as it can be to watch, this can easily build a misguided version of the reality that medical teams are faced with on a day-day basis.

This also goes for us too. Day by day we're out in the ambulance responding to calls on a regular basis and to start with just hear a voice at the end of the radio giving us information about jobs we have to attend. How much do I really know about the job of the call handler? We can easily become blinkered, in our outlook, when we get a call five minutes before the end of your twelve-hour shift. Tired, fatigued, frustrated, all the natural human emotions that one would expect in such a situation. As much as we have to make split second decisions there are others, within this industry, that also have to do the same. People we never meet face-to-face but have a huge bearing on the way that your day will go.

I can remember this one occasion when my crewmate and I were transporting a patient to hospital. We were roughly quarter of a mile away when the handling of the vehicle did not feel right. All the instruments on the dashboard were fine but something just felt a little off. When we got there I parked up the ambulance and we handed over our patient. When we returned we began to investigate to see what was wrong. On further inspection we discovered that the vehicle had a rear tyre inner puncture and, although not completely flat, the vehicle was not safe to use until repaired.

After speaking to a manager they advised that, due to it being late in the evening, we would have to await recovery. It just so happened that it was a short walk, across from the hospital, to our control room but with it being a freezing cold evening it was agreed that we should wait in the warm.

It was here that my outlook towards the men and women of the control room changed forever. As I mentioned before, we can all make assumptions about what we don't know and perhaps create a false view of what people's jobs are actually like. Nothing can build a better and more accurate picture than seeing things with your own two eyes.

The control room manager made us a hot drink and as we drank it we listened into the live 999 calls that were being received. It struck me, within seconds of the first call to come in, just how calm under pressure the staff were. For me, I meet these people who call in face-face, however, the staff here do not have that luxury. Trying to calm a caller down in real time, who is hysterical, is no easy task and all the time, whilst doing this, letting them see that you're there to help them.

For many callers it is a daunting prospect having to dial 999 and it can be hard for them to focus as they wait for the control room to answer. Callers, of course, face a bit of a roulette wheel in knowing if they will get through as quickly as they anticipate and this can increase their anxiety.

Research has shown that our ability to concentrate is reduced significantly when in a stressful situation because our brain is overloaded with information and is trying to process this in a compressed time frame. This fact alone, just shows the kind of person a call handler has to be when they are presented with multiple medical emergencies time and time again in a twelve-hour shift.

I was plugged into a call and it wasn't long before I could hear the ringing in the headset. The call was answered with, "Ambulance service – is the patient breathing", this is the standard answer to enable the call handler to establish which line of questioning is required to best help the patient. The screams that bellowed through the headset sent a shiver down my spine! I could not help but realise just how hard it is to gather information with no 'eyes in the room'. The call handler was telling the caller to calm down so to better assist the patient, to be 'our eyes in the room' and to tell us exactly what was going on.

It transpired that an elderly lady had fallen in her kitchen, banged her head on the counter, as she went down and was now unconscious. You could tell in the caller's voice how emotional she was but the calmness of the call handler helped steer her in the right direction to what was required for the patient without of course having to be there them self.

In these situations, it is like time stands still, seconds can seem like minutes and minutes seem like hours. It didn't take long for the caller to begin following the call handler's instructions. A second voice was heard in the caller's room which we were told was the patient regaining consciousness around a minute or so later.

I remember paying attention to the sounds in the room, it was almost like when you watch a movie about a submarine – the guy onboard at the radar with his headset on deciphering the sounds coming down the end of his earpiece.

You automatically try and build a mental picture, an image that can help you understand what the home or location is really like. Some of the calls can be more complicated – language barriers, young children – all those extra little difficulties that can make understanding the imminent needs of the patient that little bit harder.

In some cases there can be a scary silence on the phone line. This is often when the patient themselves have called and it is unclear if their silence is due to the patient taking a turn for the worse. Around a few minutes later I could hear the wailing of a siren in the background that gave me a sense of relief knowing that the service managed to help someone at their worst. All this had been completed with limited information other that what we were able to extract from the caller at the time.

This case fortunately had a positive outcome but for some others they're not always as lucky. I asked the call handler what it can be like when they're in the situation knowing that the case is likely not to have a good outcome. He explained it was a combination of mixed emotions, like being on a roller-coaster with each bend and turn a different emotion. He went on to say that, for some people that are unable to control their emotions under pressure, it can be very difficult especially with the nature of some of the jobs.

Each job, that had a bad outcome, left an emotional scar but that you gradually built up a layer to protect yourself from the impact of the next difficult call that came along.

As each case comes along you can start to clearly tell if it is immediately life threatening or not. It is important to keep yourself focused in the present but to also to talk about the challenging jobs afterwards if needed.

With the thought of knowing just how stressful the job role was, I was curious to see if there was a light that shone in the control room in terms of calls that lightened the mood. The call handler, I was with, said that there are some occasions when a call comes through that you find it hard to contain your laughter at the nature of the call.

One case that happened, not that long ago, came from a female caller trapped in her bath. It was suggested that her and her husband were being intimate when she somehow got one of her thumbs stuck up the tap. Like with anything, curiosity will always get the better of you – it's human nature after all.

The caller explained what he and his wife had been doing and that he tried his best to get her free but with no success. I think I would definitely have found it hard to maintain my composure but we have to be professional and the seriousness of the situation will always come first. Even though this appeared to be a humorous situation, the call handler still had ask about the height of the water, the temperature of the water and room and the circumference of her thumb. All this while the 'patient' was screaming with frustration in the background and the husband unable to contain his laughter as he is relayed the information. For me, I think I would be more worried about the reaction I would get from the wife once she was free regarding my laughter. It was a weekend evening and the crew, that were on scene, said they had been unable to remove her thumb from the tap. The only option, at this point, was for the call handler to request the assistance of the Fire and Rescue service.

I never did get the chance to ask the reaction of the Fire and Rescue call handler but I think it is safe to say that they too would have probably found it as amusing as we did.

The reaction from the wife that the Fire and Rescue service were going to have to be in attendance didn't go down well at all. We may all have been in a position of embarrassment at some point in our life and some obviously worse than others. Fortunately the wife did eventually see the funny side of the situation in the end, probably as a result of seeing that it couldn't get much worse.

By the time the job was finished the wife was fine, however, we never did find out if we could say the same about any possible repercussions to the laughter of the husband.

The unique and unexpected time I spent in the control room, that day, has taught me that one person's weakness can be another's strength and, that not only can we achieve the most amazing things, you don't necessarily need to be in the same room to do it! We all perceive our life experiences in different ways and we can all learn from another's journey. These kinds of experiences can change the outlook of all – I now have the ultimate amount of respect for the job of the emergency call handlers.

Laughter through tears is my favourite emotion.

Robert Harling (Truvy Jones in 'Steel Magnolias')

13 | Four-legged Frustration

CAN YOU TRY AND PICTURE the least perfect situation to be in? One that not only frustrates the life out of you but also one where you are laughing so hard that you could barely stand up straight as a result.

It had been a great day and all our jobs were going smoothly – the typical sort of jobs that just needed further investigation at the hospital. One by one, we assessed our patients and dropped them off at the hospital. Following the last handover I looked at the clock on the dashboard and it was just over two hours before the end of the shift. A point where you are hoping for just one last job before you went off duty. We tapped the 'Clear and Available' button on the on-board computer and began to sit and wait for another call. A few moments later we were alerted to a call approximately eight miles away. The call was on a residential caravan park for a patient in their seventies with chest pain.

Call outs for patients with chest pain is a very common, however, what can seem sinister on the face of it, can sometimes turn out to be of no consequence after the patient has been assessed.

Strains from lifting heavy objects, falls or even things such as patients with an ongoing cough can cause this type of pain but nothing is ever 'off the table' until the patient has been fully assessed.

When we got to the location we were greeted by a member of the site's security staff who showed us, on a map, the exact location of the patient's chalet. As we stopped outside, we observed there was a Community First Responder's car also outside the home. These volunteers are worth their weight in gold – people that all want to make a difference in their community.

My crewmate knocked on the door and we were greeted by the First Responder who introduced us to the patient. We learnt that the patient had a history of high blood pressure and that she had been suffering, on and off, chest pain since the morning and, as it had not gone away, had called 999.

We began to assess the patient when, all of a sudden, a little dog ran into the room and began to franticly run around wanting a good fuss to be made of it. It's quite a regular occurrence for us to see pets in patient's homes – in fact the control room will often ask the patient to lock their dogs away just to make sure it's safe for the crew.

It was a lovely dog, rolling around and wagging its hips from side to side, all with a clear intention to show it wanted to be friends. The patient told us just how long she had the dog, it was not a young dog but it had the energy of one that was equivalent of a young puppy.

All the checks were fine after performing a complete assessment with no obvious indicator of an immediate heart attack taking place. Of course she needed further investigation to rule anything else out which meant we would have to take her to hospital. I started to complete the paperwork to make things quicker and smoother for the handover. My crewmate and the First Responder said that they will take the equipment out to the ambulance ready for the journey.

Time was passing and then it suddenly dawned on me that my crewmate and the First Responder had not returned. All of a sudden my crewmate came running back in and asked for my help. Puzzled, I couldn't help but think to myself, "What in the world has happened?". She had a look of horror on her face and also one that seemed to say that she wanted the ground to open up under her feet and consume her on the spot.

As I made my way to the front door, I could hear a roar of laughter out in the car park. By the time I had got to the door my crewmate had disappeared again. I asked the First Responder where she was. Laughing, she pointed behind the caravan and said that she will watch the patient whilst I go and help. I was still puzzled and no wiser as to what in the world was happening.

I walked between the caravans to be confronted by a huge open field. It had to be at least half a mile wide and about half as long. It was dark so had to call out to my crewmate to try and locate where she was. I could hear the faint sound of a voice in the distance. This was when I instantly fell to my knees with laughter as well as shock.

What had happened was that, when they both had gone outside to the ambulance, the patient's dog had bolted for the door at the same time. Unbeknown to them it had made a dash for the field and off into the darkness. Apparently, it was the sound of its collar that drew their attention which initiated the chase for retrieval.

Looking across the field I could just make out the shape of a human body diving in a frantic leap in an attempt to catch the dog. The dog then stopped ten yards ahead and ran around my crewmate in circles of sheer delight at the thought that this unusual behaviour was a late-night game.

I could hear her shouting up the field calling the dog, "Please come back", even offering it a treat that she had found in the property when she came back to ask for my help. I couldn't compose myself for laughing so much. Seeing my crewmate dive in the distance and the same time thinking of just how long they had been trying to catch it was making my stomach hurt all the more.

We had already been on scene some considerable time. After a certain point the control room will often call us to check on our welfare and, with it being late at night, they will want to ensure that nothing is wrong as well as log any kind of delay.

I had joined in the chase to catch the dog and we were all running around the field – the dog going one way and me the other. The further it ran away the harder it was to try and keep eyes on it. I looked back in the direction we had come to discover we were getting further and further away from the caravan site. I managed to get within inches of the dog with bribing it with a treat but, just as I was about to dive and catch it, my radio went off scaring the bloody hell out of me. The dog leapt up in the air, whilst cocking its head to one side, as if to say what the hell are you doing?

I answered the radio but the sound of my voice clearly showed how out of breath I was. Trying to compose my laughter, I explained that the patient was fine, but unfortunately, we were chasing a runaway dog across a field with no success of catching it.

There was a weird kind of pause on the radio. When they began speaking again, you could tell by the sound of their voice, they too were trying to contain their laughter – but equally doing their best to be professional at the same time.

It had been raining slightly so wasn't a perfect dry night and the ground was a little damp. Every time we made a lunge at the dog, to catch it, we skidded on the wet grass.

We devised a plan, to try and walk in a certain direction that would make the dog run closer to where it had come from. As we were doing this the security guard came to join us. He said, that he'd been standing watching us from the security hut and never seen anything so funny – he hadn't come over to help as he'd been helpless with laughter.

So there we were... my crewmate, myself and the security guard, all three of us running around this field in the dark chasing this dog. I definitely think the dog was finding it just as funny as we were.

As we approached an area closer to the caravan, I could hear the patient shouting out that they are not going to hospital unless the dog was caught. Just the thought of how long this running around had been going on was mind-blowing.

We were now eventually making some progress and, as we got closer to the caravan site, my crewmate had managed to sneak up on the dog – just enough to grab a hold of it. This was obviously met with a frantic struggle by the dog who tried to make a last-ditch attempt to get to freedom again.

A feeling of relief came over me, I was exhausted, to think how long my crewmate had been diving around on a field still makes me laugh to this day. The dog was safely returned and shut away just to be sure.

The patient was eventually conveyed to hospital. A follow-up about the patient was that the chest pain, thankfully, was not due to a cardiac condition.

Every time I have been back to that residential caravan park, I'm still in hysterics just as I was that night. They say that a dog is a man's best friend but an open field in the dark certainly didn't make it the case that night.

As long as you laugh at yourself,
you will never cease to be amused.

Unknown

14 | Light Through the Tunnel

HAVE ENCOUNTERED, over the course of my career, many different personalities, from funny, rude, abrupt to the very well-to-do.

With the job, being what it is, you never know who you're going to come into contact with – a kind of roulette. When you knock on a door you do not know who is going to greet you on the other side.

Despite the reasons for our attendance, each and every patient has one thing in common and that is for us to be at our best when they're at their worst. We will always aim to do our upmost to deliver the best level of care and to the highest standard, however, not everyone will want us to treat them the same due to their different outlook on life.

One thing for certain is that we will encounter laughter, tears, excitement and bereavement but each of us will handle these differently. I guess the reason for this is our upbringing, our exposure to various life events and the fact we can only really compare a current situation to our past experiences.

As paramedics we are clinically autonomous and have to make quick decisions based on our experience and knowledge. No two patients will be the same even if they appear to have similar conditions. For example if two separate patients have called in to say they are experiencing breathing difficulties, the likelihood is that their treatment will be completely different.

It was the middle of the summer, a bright beautiful day and very hot. A lot of the calls we had been receiving that day had been from patient's not staying hydrated. When you attend many calls about similar conditions, it is important not to become complacent – in doing so, it can be very easy to overlook things that you would normally see and this could be hazardous to the treatment and outcome of the patient.

We received a call for a gentleman who said that he was feeling generally unwell. On the face of it, this could be interpreted as many different things. Upon arrival, my crewmate and I were greeted and asked to come inside. We followed the patient through to his lounge and sat together to have a chat.

My initial observation was that there were many empty beer cans strewn about the floor. I looked over into the kitchen and noticed a lot of empty microwave food packets lying about on the kitchen work surfaces. It was very evident that the patient was not coping. However, we had only just entered the home and, we now needed to get to the bottom of why he had called.

My crewmate asked how we could help but he just said that he doesn't feel well and wasn't sure what to do. When asked if he could explain a bit further, he said that he had been feeling very mentally unwell and 'all over the place'. This had led him on a downward spiral and not able to reach the place he had been at.

It was important at this point to try and understand. To listen to his story and to see just how we could try and help where possible. He explained that his mother had passed away two years prior and, being very close to her, could not get over this and was also finding it difficult to engage sociably.

Looking around the room, I saw that the furniture was very dated. The only way I can explain it is that it was as if you placed a 30-year-old man in a room with décor from the 1950's. Following more conversation, he went on to tell us that both he and his mother had been born in the home.

The level of connection, with his family home and environment, was very clear. I tried to think of myself in his position and understood the deep sense of history a home can have for someone.

Trying to relate to the patient better, I began going through their medical history. This is normal practice that enables us to have a broader knowledge and understanding that helps us to move forward in treating the patient.

I'm not sure why but there was something about the way the patient was talking that just didn't sit right with me. I don't know what made me observe this but call it a 'gut feeling' or possibly just an instinct and a result of speaking to so many people on a regular basis.

When I enquired about his regular medications he asked me to get his repeat prescription list from his bedroom. I made my way to the door and swung it open. I was suddenly confronted with a huge collection of wall-to-wall football memorabilia and his team's colours as far as the eye could see.

T-shirts, match programmes, photos as well as cups, all laid out showing an immense dedication and love for football. We all have our passions in life, some of us can let it take over our lives and get so absorbed in it that we will go to any lengths to fulfil our passion.

I managed to locate the prescription. The medications that were listed showed that the patient had been having difficulty in sleeping and also suffered from anxiety. A combination that can spiral out of control should it not be managed properly.

Returning to the lounge, I managed to use what I had just seen in his bedroom as a good point of conversation. My aim was to try and get the patient to open up a bit more. With all my observations it was clear that the patient was suffering with depression. This can be a very dark place for some and can be extremely difficult to talk to a complete stranger let alone for the person trying to counsel them to relate to anything that maybe going on in their life.

In these situations, we are not the 'keeper of all answers', we just have to try and have a clear head and build a sensible picture as to the most practical way forward.

I began to ask him about his love of football and mentioned that it was quite the collection he had built. He told me how much of a fan he is of the club that he supports. They were a premier league team and he attended every away game. He was a dedicated fan and got so much fulfilment of feeling a part of the team.

He told me that he had built a social media fan page for the team. As he began to discuss this he picked up an iPad and showed me the page. There were hundreds of thousands of followers.

I have seen some dedication in my time but this was on another level. As I sat there with him I noticed some pictures on the wall, signed pictures with him and some of the team from times he had spent at various matchs.

The conversation had really begun to pick up pace. Now I felt it was the right time to drill deeper into what was really going on in his life to cause an ambulance crew to attend.

It was a difficult thing to ask but the only thing I could think of was why he no longer attended the matches. When prompted, he started to tell me about the loss of his mother, a few years before, and the subsequent bereavement he had suffered. Now looking around the room this all began to make so much sense.

The out-dated décor, the furniture and the fact the patient lived in this kind of environment had brought it all together for me. Nothing can prepare you for a loss of a loved one, especially someone so close to you such as a parent. He explained that his mother was his best friend and that they did everything together, shopping, walks to town as well as trips to see family.

Considering their age and relationship, some may see this was an unhealthy situation but, for someone who has never married with a limited family, it was marvellous to hear about their beautiful friendship.

He told me that since his loss that it slowly came about that he had no drive or desire to do anything and this was the commencement of his downward spiral. Once he started to go downhill mentally, he lost all hope of getting back to engaging in life again. The light that was at the end of the tunnel became further and further away.

There are many different views about depression, some people say it is a cry for attention or faked as an excuse to just do nothing. However, when you see the pain in the eyes of someone who is suffering from depression, with whatever ordeal they've endured, it is hard to ignore.

Regardless of your outlook on life, everybody's journey is different and it's not for anyone else to judge – and for the one's that do, this can make things a lot worse about the way a person is already feeling.

I had to be quite forceful in the way that I asked the next few questions, by this, I mean as to where he was mentally at this present time. Some may just feel low, others may have had serious suicidal thoughts that later go away. Some have a carefully thought out plan with the means to carry it out, without others knowing, only to be discovered later by their nearest and dearest.

As he had asked for an ambulance, I suspected that things were really bad. As I slowly and tentatively started to speak to him he finally told me that he could not go on. He just wanted to be in a place that made him happy. He had the intention of taking a serious overdose. However, when he went to carry this out, something made him stop. We asked him what it was that made him think twice and carrying through with it.

He wanted to be a part of football again and to have the courage to leave the house which he rarely had done over the last two years. When hearing him talk about football you could hear the passion in his voice. I'm not a huge football fan at all but I could relate to be completely passionate about something I love. It was clear that if something was not done, to support him, this great man would soon no longer be with us.

I asked him how he would feel if he was able to go and see a game and to be amongst others who he used to see on a regular basis. The look on the face said it all.

We all love to share stories about various events that have happened in our life. Memories that we have made together with family and friends be it funny or sad. In this young man's case they were memories of iconic football games he had attended with his mates and that had made him happy. As he spoke about this, you could see his spirits were being lifted.

He carried on to tell us that all of his worries and fears would just fade away, for 90 minutes, if he could see his team play again. The dark thoughts, that had plagued him since his mother's death, would no longer be at the forefront of his mind.

I was conscious of the fact that, regardless if he went to hospital or not, he would need that boost of confidence to help him engage back into society again.

Unbeknown to the patient, I had a family friend who used to play for the very club that he was a fan of. He used to play way back in the 1950's as part of their academy. Throughout his football life he had played with people such as Martin Peters, John Bond and Harry Redknapp. I had known this player and his partner for many years. Over the years I have chatted to many football fans and knew how it can be a true passion for many people.

The young guy said that he did not wish to go to hospital – he felt that he just wanted to chat and the fact that we took the time listen he felt a lot better. Hearing him say that was really positive and he said that he was not going to do anything stupid.

I felt like I wanted to give him an extra boost, to at least try and get him back into society again and back to where he once was a few years before.

I made an excuse to pop outside to the ambulance. I had the idea to ring my friend and explain that I had a patient who is a huge fan of the club that he used to play with. I obviously could not divulge any information about the young guy nor could I mention any other aspect of what was going on in his life.

When I rang, his partner answered the phone. I asked if he was there and if I could speak with him. When he came to the phone I explained that a huge fan would love to have the opportunity to talk about the club with a former player. He said he would be delighted and would be honoured to speak with someone who was such a huge fan. Although the patient was not aware of the call, I had just made, I knew he would be made up to have the conversation.

What really strikes me about the older generation is how things were so different years ago. My football player friend often tells me stories about how he used to play first thing in the morning, get changed and then straight off to work at a paper factory. As a player he only got £1.50 plus expenses – a world apart from the vast sums of money players get today. It's quite evident how the modern game of football has changed over the years and is now treated, predominately, as a business.

I was still on the phone, with my friend, as I returned to the house. I went up to the young guy and began to tell him what I had just been up to.

I explained that I was friends with a former player of his favourite team and that he played for the club many years ago. He straight away knew who I was talking about when I mentioned his name. Considering his knowledge, for the sport, how could he not know who he was?

I asked if he would like to talk to him and that I would love to give him the boost and confidence to take that step to get back to what he loves so much.

I handed the phone over. I could see his hand shaking as he took the phone from me. Listening to him talk, it was as if he had not long come back from a match. As he spoke I felt a slight apprehension wondering if I had really put him in contact with the right person. He began to ask some questions, that I guess, only a real player would have been able to answer properly. Positive answers came back as quickly as the questions were asked. The young football fan looked at me and said, "It is him!". The look on his face said it all.

They spoke for a good fifteen minutes and this was enough time for my crewmate and I to do a referral to the patients GP. We wanted to ensure that he got the support he so desperately deserved. We could see the young man was a very private person but the call he had made that day, asking for help, was a blessing in disguise.

We understandably couldn't stay there forever and a short time later he ended the call. The young guy now looked like a different person. Not only was he laughing and chatting about the things he had discussed on the phone, he started talking about trailers he had seen on the TV for upcoming matches.

This was a job that will sit with me for a long time. We very rarely get to see how a patient's life turns out but can only hope that this brief moment, in his life, gave him the boost to get him back on track.

As paramedics we often glimpse a small snapshot into the lives of our patients. Some sad, some happy, others funny, so to see such a positive transition in this young guy, over the course of a just a few hours, really made me see just why I love this job so much.

I will always be thankful for the help my friend and his partner gave that day. Friends are so important when you're down and I truly hope that, the young guy we saw that day, gets to spend time back at the club with the friends he so badly missed.

Each one of us can make a difference.
Together we make a change.

Barbara Mikulski

15 | A World Apart

SOMETIMES we may look back on our lives and reflect on how honest we have been with ourselves as to how good or bad things have gone over time.

We may have all gone through some challenges and troubles in our life, so it is important to identify a learning point – not only to use as a foundation for moving forward but also to help learn from each other so that this can be used as a form of support.

I would never, in a million years, have thought of myself in the role that I now have. To be honest, I would not have seen myself being up to the role and certainly not the confidence to go out there in the world and be an intervenor between fate and circumstance where someone is at their worst.

You often hear the phrase 'anything is possible' – a phrase that became all too familiar as time began to pass. Having enough confidence in our day-day lives, to achieve our goals that we set ourselves, can be difficult. We can all lack confidence at times, in some capacity, whether it relates to interviews, starting new tasks or in trying to communicate when making new friends.

Being in the job as long as I have has taught me that, no matter the medical emergency, people's lives can really change forever and move forward in a positive way. You only have to look at the story of the lady I treated who survived a cardiac arrest or the incident of having a firearm pointed at my head.

All these things can seriously affect an individual and can create a shockwave in various aspects of their life. They can also, in turn, affect the people around them such as their nearest and dearest.

I grew up in a culture that was very much took the attitude of 'taking it on the chin' and to move on with your life. As the years have gone by it now seems to be the complete opposite and more for promoting, "It's OK to not be OK".

With poor mental health being on the rise it is important to observe, that no matter the background, we're only going to break the stigma of talking about mental ill health if we can accept that everyone's story is unique. We have to understand that what will affect someone one way, can affect the next person completely differently.

For a long time I didn't notice that I was suffering with a poor mental health. It was only due to a sympathetic work colleague, picking up on things, that made me look at myself objectively. I learnt quite quickly, that every bad thing that happens in our lives will form a kind of emotional scar – a scar that forms a layer that partly covers your emotions to help protect you in the future. The problem is, in doing so, it can also create an emotional numbness and distance you from other aspects you encounter through your journey in life.

The road to recovery, for sufferers of poor mental health, can be a long-protracted journey. The biggest thing is to try to accept that you have a problem. For a while I was naive and too proud to face up to things. It was not until it was pointed out to me that, I was showing signs of depression, I began to take it seriously and take a long hard look at myself.

That good look in the mirror, as they say, showed that I had become withdrawn from the day-day things that I used to do on a regular basis. For me it was not going to the gym or socialising with my friends. Was this my mind's defence mechanism kicking in? As the weeks and months passed by it was more and more evident that this was in fact the case. The lack of contact with people happened so gradually that, before long, the change had become a world apart from where I was to begin with.

The brain is a marvellous organ that can process vast amounts of information and can react at lightning speed such as in the fight or flight response when confronted with a difficult situation. From an initial ordeal, you may have experienced, right the way through to the protective mechanism you use when you haven't confronted your demons.

The battle with depression is different for everyone. A person's attitude to their illness, and ability to pull through, is a key factor in getting better. Having a goal to focus on has been really important to me. I found that by writing things down, not only have I been able to make sense of what I've faced, I was also able to pull the situation apart to better understand every detail.

This kind of self-therapy has aided me in writing this book – not only to help myself but also to open up and help others in a way that they may be able to relate to. My hope is that in writing this book it may help people to have a deeper understanding of a paramedic's job and the life and death emergency situations we experience in the real world.

We all come into contact, whatever job we do, with a whole range of people in everyday life. Whether it is face-to-face, by phone, by email or a video call – we all have a view on the way people are treated or the way they treat us.

My real 'take home' message from all of this is that we need to understand ourselves better and manage our health both physically and mentally. I never thought I would be in the position where I would be able to save the life of a friend – to see a decline in mental health of a young guy one day and the next helping to save him by way of support and intervention.

I believe that intervening in those situations where we can, and going the extra mile, we can all learn a lot from the experience. To see how much, or even how little people have really does make you think. What can be simple gesture of support, on the face of it, can and will mean the world to the person you are helping.

It was difficult to come to terms with the realisation that I was suffering with my mental health – the stigma that's attached to it can make you feel judged by those who you have always known and hoped were your friends.

Talking to a stranger seemed weird to begin with, to open up with someone who you might assume, at a first meeting, had no idea how you were feeling. If you're fortunate though, like I was, you might meet a person who can begin a conversation in a good way, a sort of 'ice breaker', that might pave the way for your road to recovery.

I remember my 'ice breaker' question was, "What did I like do as a pastime?" and then, "How often do you do it?", which led on to me saying, "Not as much as I would like". It was a clever opening line that engaged me in talking about something I had a passion for. The lady who helped me was lovely and had a calming influence in the way she spoke but mainly she just listened. She took an impartial stance and was non-judgemental.

Before long I had spoken to her about a large chapter in my life without knowing that, although it formed a multi-faceted puzzle, it was gradually linking together by way of another confusing and complicated chapter of emotions.

Was it right to talk to someone? – I don't know. To lay out all those feelings for others to see – to bare all. It didn't feel right to start with. I remember just giving little bits away to smooth out the conversation and perhaps only tell her what I thought she wanted to hear.

I had to keep reminding myself that, this kind lady, was not my enemy, not someone that will expose my deepest thoughts and emotions to the world around me. Of course this is exactly what I have done, right here. I now know, that the only way things can change, is for all to know that, "It's OK to not feel OK" – just as the mental health advert says.

Now that I began to explain everything, about the worries and fears in my life, I could slowly see a plan forming that would help me feel better. The sleepless nights I used to have begun to reduce. I now understand just how important it was for me to make sense of my journey up to this point and that I was not alone in the world.
Just that thought was enough for me to ditch the feeling of being too proud but still hold my head up in positive determination in getting on with my life.

My goal and aspiration of becoming a paramedic was a great focus for me in looking to the future – after all, I was most definitely going to encounter many people in a similar position that I had been in.

Not only was talking essential on the road to recovery but also the skill of listening was just as important. Understanding how people are feeling and the coping mechanisms they use, to aid their journey, was invaluable. My grandfather always told me that you can't buy practical experience. This statement is so true – not something I would have appreciated all those years ago but something that has remained with me.

The usual course of events, in my day-to-day job, is to respond quickly to help others who are in trouble, so it was a surprise to me and felt strange when I was the one that needed help this time. There is a lot to be said for appreciating the simple things in life and, by opening up to a complete stranger, I had learnt a life lesson that was worth more to me than I could have hoped for.

Months past and I could see, as well as feel, the difference in myself. I was less fatigued, had more energy and looked forward to making the best of the day. I no longer wanted to be a recluse as I had done on many occasions before.

If it wasn't for the people that meant the most to me, in my life, I could not imagine how things could have turned out. But life is about understanding, being able to comprehend just how important some situations can be in life.

I am the father of an autistic son. He is, at the time of writing this, six years of age – unfortunately he has no concept of how serious the world is around him. Some people may read this and think, "Nor does any six-year-old at this point in their life". He has no sense of danger or fear and his emotional detachment in certain situations can cause him all sorts of problems. Generally we are all aware of our actions towards others, sensitive to their feelings and responses – these are important social skills inherent in most of us. However, some people do not have that capability. Observing this has helped me in supporting him and to better grasp his leaning and understanding. This has also taught me how relevant this is in our interaction with each other.

Feelings of darkness and despair can be an everyday occurrence for some people but can also have a serious and profound effect on others if we allow it to. It can be easy to fall by the wayside in a downward spiral that gains momentum with no traction to stop. For those who have not been there, it is a scary and dark place. Luckily for me it was picked up early, early enough that I didn't slip too far down into an abyss. I can only try to explain my own personal experience of alienation, in some kind of way, to others who are slipping even further than I did. However, the reality is, I can only imagine what they have endured on their journey to be where they are today.

Fortunately there is a lot of help out there now, especially post Covid-19. The global experience of a pandemic meant that, for many of us, the only way to avoid contracting the virus was to stay at home for prolonged periods of time. As a result this brought about a detachment from our family and friends and, for some people, even dissociation from reality. We had lost that social physical connection that forms part of our everyday life. I think we should all take a moment to reflect on how we felt, or would have felt, not being able to engage with the people around us.

Fortunately I am now in a much better place and have set myself the goal to make each day count – to be the best that I can be and help others to do the same. I've been through some dark days in my life but, thanks to the people who mean the most to me, I have managed to realise my dreams of becoming a paramedic. This will always be a constant reminder to me of the man I have become today.

It is good to have an end to journey toward, but it is the journey that matters, in the end.

Ernest Hemingway